THE GUARDED ONE

A Child's Journey Through War

by Lindiwe Magaya

A wholly owned subsidiary of **TBN**

The Guarded One: A Child's Journey Through War

Trilogy Christian Publishers A Wholly Owned Subsidiary of Trinity Broadcasting Network

2442 Michelle Drive Tustin, CA 92780

For information about special discounts for bulk purchases, please contact Trilogy Christian Publishing.

Manufactured in the United States of America

10 9 8 7 6 5 4 3 2 1

Library of Congress Cataloging-in-Publication Data is available.

ISBN: 978-1-68556-615-9

E-ISBN: 978-1-68556-616-6

Dedication

To my father, Jonathan Jonah, and mother, Thabiso. Thank you for the lifelong lessons you imparted. This is in your honor.

Acknowledgments

This work would not be complete without the help and support of my village. To my siblings, thank you for letting me glean from you. You have stood by me and been a pillar of support from the time I was born. Thank you for journeying with me in bringing this work to fruition.

My extended family, both maternal and paternal, have been my village and my source of support. Thank you, cousins Nothani and Tsatsi Maphosa, aunties Lineo Njini, Jelitha, and Juliet Maphosa, Moratiwa Gazi (Abigail Mabetha), Sithabile Moyo, and Bhuzhwa (Bourgeoisie).

Reverend Rodgers Dube, Patience Mlotshwa, Daisy, Joyce Nyathi, and Priscilla Mtungwa Ndlovu, thank you for your wealth of knowledge as you helped me understand and interpret circumstances revealed in this work.

To my preschool teacher, Mrs. Sejo Mkandla, and first-grade teacher, Mrs. Siyengo Siwawa, thank you for the foundation you laid. It paid dividends.

Sihlangu Dlodlo, Dr. Barbara Makhalisa Nkala, and Dr. Gloria Edwards, thank you for taking time from your busy schedule to review my work and provide an in-depth and much-needed feedback. Your expertise is invaluable.

To my husband Amu, daughter Thandi Jessica, and son Unalenna (Unah) for your unwavering support and encouragement as I was penning this story, thank you. To my nephews and nieces, thank you for your support.

To my fellow *kijanas*, Refiloe Nondo, Sikhanyiso Jamela, Sukoluhle Ncube, and Alice Ngwenya, what can I say? Our story has finally come alive. This is to you and to all the *kijanas* out there.

Last but most importantly, I would like to extend my sincere gratitude to Trilogy Christian Publishing for believing in my work and bringing it to life. Thank you for your guidance.

Table of Contents

Prologue

Like many families in Zimbabwe in the 1970s, my family and I lived in the city while owning a home in the rural areas or reservations, as they were called. We would visit our rural home in the Gwanda area of Sengezane during the school holidays, particularly the December-January and the April-May period. This was a great time to be in the rural area for several reasons. The planting of crops took place during the December-January period, while the harvesting took place during the April-May holiday. Both school holidays were enjoyable as they ushered in the rains and a harvest, and three of my favorite holidays, Christmas, New Year, and Easter. This was a time to enjoy free crops and wild fruit that were not otherwise easily available in the city. It was a great time for me to show off my city girl skills and beautiful clothes.

Although I enjoyed the visit to our rural home, I was content with living in the city and just visiting the rural area for the holidays. I considered myself a city girl. My life, however, was shaped by these places I came to call my home during my early years of development.

It was at Ross Camp in Bulawayo, also known as the city of Kings, that memory of my life begins. My life as a five-year-old to a seven-year-old can be described as both challenging and exciting. Ross Camp was one of the largest police camps in the country at the time. It housed the administrative offices that served most of the townships on the western side of Bulawayo. It was rent-free housing provided for police officers and their families. Larger families like mine occupied four-roomed houses, with two bedrooms, a lounge, and a kitchen. Uncle Amon and Aunt Jelitha, Cousin Anna, and Elizabeth (my babysitter) were part of my extended family that shared this humble home with us.

The toilets were attached outside the houses as an afterthought, in my judgment. These toilets served as both toilets and bathrooms. Public toilets were also available along with single household blocks or unmarried person quarters and always had a stench that would linger in the air for hours—that of a combination of green vegetables, onions, and beans. Or so I thought as a five-year-old. Stories of stray black cats posing as witches and wizards circulated, and as a result, I was afraid of using the toilet at night.

Our Ross Camp was a "perfect" world to raise a child,

with hardly any crime since it was a police camp. There was law and order. We knew what time to go to the only available public swimming pool and the playground. We knew where to play and when to go home for supper. We knew when to go to the Beit Hall for entertainment and when to go home. We knew where to hunt for locusts and where to make a fire and roast them. We enjoyed that security and order. It was part of us. It formed us. It dictated our lives.

Perfect as our Ross Camp appeared, the swimming pool and playground days ushered in my first encounter with racism. At Ross Camp, apartheid-style, White officers had their residences on the south-eastern side of the camp, away from our crowded Black side of the camp. We shared a few facilities like the swimming pool, playground, and Beit Hall, where White children would try to keep us out by bullying and/or pelting us with stones. Sometimes we would scurry and collect our belongings and leave before our time was up. Other times, we would stand our ground and continue as if their pelting was an insignificant matter. There is one time, however, when some Black children returned fire by throwing stones back at the White children. That behavior resulted in Black children being banned for some time from enjoying the swimming pool and the playground. It seemed acceptable at the time to have one group bully another and not the other way around.

The rise of African nationalism in the early 1960s was the beginning of the end of the British minority rule in Southern Africa. As predicted by the then British Prime Minister Harold Macmillan in his speech in Cape Town on February 3, 1960 (Dubow, 2013), "winds of change" were sweeping across the southern African continent and would be unstoppable. In Zimbabwe, then Rhodesia, ominous clouds of national political consciousness were looming across the country, an indication that a storm was brewing. This storm led to the Zimbabwe War of Liberation, also known as the Rhodesian Bush War, which pounded the country from 1964 to 1979.

I was born in December of 1965, a year after the beginning of that war, fought by many people, young and old, from different fronts both in and outside Zimbabwe. There are many unsung heroes whose stories have not been told and may never be heard. It is important to acknowledge their story as part of Zimbabwean history that cannot be ignored. My story is part of that history.

My mother and father birthed six children: two boys and four girls. Three of the siblings, Emmanuel, Orpha, and Shepherd, were the older ones, while Nhlanhla, Thando, and I, Lindiwe, were the younger ones. I am the youngest of the siblings. My full name Lindiwe is a girl name meaning the guarded or protected one. My mother gave me that name in prayer that God would keep watch over me and guard me. My name also means the awaited one. Although both meanings would have worked, my mother's prayer was for the Almighty to keep watch over me. A beautiful name indeed. This name was also prophetic, as it proved over and over in my life how God would watch over me. It is my journey as the guarded one that has compelled me to pen my story about the realities of surviving a war as a child.

As my family and I navigated through the Zimbabwe War of Liberation, we experienced both harrowing and commemorative events. These events shaped and molded me. It is through my childhood eyes that I perceived how situations, decisions, and changes, eventually played out on each family member. It is through my eyes, as a child, that my story is told. Had I been an adult, I would have had a different perspective. A constant flashback of these events has motivated me to pen my story, my journey, and hope it brings a smile, a chuckle, and a tear. It is my hope that this narrative will inspire, motivate, educate, and bring hope to the hopeless. I have never walked alone, and I hope no one must walk alone. My journey could not be complete without my immediate and extended family, friends, foes, and my village. It is their story that brings mine to life.

Part I: The Preparation

Chapter 1

The Matriarch

As early as I could remember, the bond that I shared with my mother, Thabiso Mabanga, was unbreakable. She was my pillar. As the oldest of her three siblings, Lineo (Lynn), Roselynn, and Khuthatso, and raised by a single mother, our maternal grandmother Matlakala Elina Java Mabanga, she was resilient and focused. She was educated by Evangelical Lutheran Church missionaries who understood the effects of poverty on academic achievement. The missionaries had identified her as an intelligent girl who needed financial support. They had provided scholarships for her to complete her secondary and tertiary education. She had graduated as a primary school teacher and taught in several neighboring schools, both in the city and in the rural area. She was one of the well-known success stories in the Gwanda region at the time, and she became the pride of the region. As a behavioral psychologist, she taught juvenile delinquents who were in detention at Patsy Ibbotson Remand Home in Bulawayo.

Even with those six children, two years apart, my mother still looked as beautiful and slim as ever. She had birthed six children within a span of ten years! She is the type that would put on any type of clothing, and it would still fit perfectly. Her slender body, with beautiful curves, and her sumptuous dark lips and delicate brown eyes presented a unique and glorious beauty. She is the type that people would say, "Ah, God took His time to create this heavenly beauty!" She was gorgeous by all standards. However, it is not this outward beauty that defined her. Her heart and character spoke volumes of the person she was.

From left to right: Emmanuel, Dad with Thando, Nhlanhla, Elizabeth (our baby sitter), Orpha, Shepherd, Mom, me (the baby), and Anna (my cousin).

My mother was the quiet type compared to my dad. I guess the responsibilities of keeping up with six children and a job as a teacher bore on her shoulders. Regardless of the responsibilities, she was the wisest, kindest, and most compassionate person I ever knew. Words of encouragement and wisdom oozed from her kind heart through her mouth, building self-esteem and confidence in the dejected.

As a selfless and cheerful giver, we compared her to *ifefe* (a roller), one of the most colorful and beautiful birds in Zimbabwe. A folktale is told in my isiNdebele language of animals and birds asking for *ifefe's* feathers to build their nests. *Ifefe* gave them, but they kept asking for more, genuinely or out of greed. After a while, *ifefe* realized she had barely any feathers left. The moral of the story is that some people take advantage of one's kindness and abuse those who are selfless givers. As a selfless giver, my mother would also guard against such ingenious and selfish people.

I never forget one time, when my mother boarded the village bus after her meeting in the city. She had brought three loaves of bread as part of the grocery. We had waited for her at the bus station. On the way home, we had passed through some homesteads where she was distributing bread to those who were underprivileged. By the time we got home, she had cut in half the last loaf. Bearing in mind that availability of bread and resources was limited in our rural village, this was an incredible display of kindness and selflessness that was forever engraved in my mind.

One thing she could not tolerate, however, was being taken advantage of. Because she was a quiet and kind person, some people would find it easy to take advantage of her kindness, like in the *ifefe* folklore. Although known as someone with patience, once crossed, there was no going back.

I am reminded of a time when her sister Lineo, who lived in Msiningira with her husband Phil, and their children, Doug and Jon, visited us at our village in Sengezane. My mother had prepared the choicest chicken as a treat for her sister. Being the greatest cook she was, she made sure she spiced that chicken to the best of her knowledge. Just as she was ready to serve so she and her sister could share the plate (which was the cultural norm), one of our village neighbors showed up.

Culturally, when an uninvited guest shows up, the "host" is supposed to offer the uninvited guest something to eat. The belief is that the "guest" is a passerby; he or she will eat just a little bit. Due to that cultural background, Mother extended an invitation to this neighbor to join her and Aunt Lynn for lunch. The neighbor gladly washed her hands and joined them. Given that the neighbor's home was close by and that my mother was entertaining her sister, this neighbor would have politely declined the invitation. That was the expectation, but this neighbor decided to go against the norm and join my mother and aunt as they shared lunch.

Mother had specifically chosen several chicken pieces for her sister as the invited guest. The pieces included a drumstick, a thigh, and the back. NaSikhangele, intoxicated by the aroma caused by my mother's cooking, was talking nonstop and laughing at the top of her voice. Salivating for this mouthwatering dish, she had reached out and picked a drumstick. My mother stopped NaSikhangele in her tracks.

"Put my young sister's drumstick down back into the plate right now! How dare you pick her drumstick! That's my young sister's drumstick!"

Caught completely by surprise, the neighbor had quickly put the drumstick back into the plate in shock and embarrassment. In our isiNdebele language, drumsticks are

21

translated as thighs. When translated from our isiNdebele language into the English language, it would sound like my aunt Lineo's thigh was the one that was on the plate, yet my mother was referring to the piece that was specifically designated for my aunt. In isiNdebele language, this is how it is presented:

"Buyisela umlenze womnawami kathesi so!" (Put back my sister's thigh right now!)

"Of all the pieces you could choose, why get the choicest? You come here when you know well that my sister is here visiting and I'm seeing her for the first time in a long time, and you invite yourself. I am not having that! There are other smaller chicken pieces and the gravy that you can enjoy."

Once my mother's temper was triggered, she would bring back to memory everything that an offender would have said or done a century ago, and you would wonder how she remembered them. Aunt Lineo had to ask her to calm down. We laughed at that incident for the longest time.

**From left to right: Aunt Lineo, her two sons
Doug and Jon, and my mom.**

We inherited an unruly gene of tonsillitis from our
mother's side of the family. She herself had suffered from
that curse. Her brood constantly suffered from tonsillitis,
which kept her on edge most of the time. Sometimes it
would be one child, and other times it would be the last
three children. We were constant visitors at the Mzilikazi
clinic in Bulawayo and faced the wrath of Nurse Nsingo

and her injections, jabs, or shots. Unfortunately, it was risky to have tonsils removed at the time. So, we lived with them and hoped to outgrow them at some point and never pass them on to the next generation. Ah, injections!

My mother's belief in me gave me confidence and built my self-esteem. Her love and support provided me with a solid foundation that would carry me through my life.

Chapter 2

The Actress

With a family of overachievers, they dominated me, and I stood no chance to be heard. I was always watching, listening, and learning. I had to find an outlet to unleash my potential. The only outlet at my disposal was at school or with my friends. I used those outlets effectively.

I was plagued with nicknames bestowed on me by my big brother Emmanuel, Uncle Amon, and others. My name is Lindiwe, which means the Guarded One. I was given my name by my mother in her belief that I was guarded by God. In my older days, my mother would occasionally complete the name by saying, "LindiweyiNkosi," the One Guarded by the Lord. I have been called by nicknames derived from my name, such as Li (Lee), Lindi (Lindie/Lindy), MaLi.

Besides the ones derived from my name, I have had nicknames derived from my personality. One such nickname was *"uMahlakanipheni,"* the Clever One or the trickster. I earned this name due to my ability to memorize and dramatize a simple rhyme, poem, or song. For some reason, my performance would somehow catch the attention of my "audience" and would earn me nicknames. I would memorize the contents page of an English bedtime story even without understanding what the words meant. English was my second language. I would sing a simple song or a rhyme and dramatize it.

I would also be called by nicknames of clever animals like the hare and the rabbit. One nickname that stands out is *"Mvundla-Tsuro"* (Hare). This is a combination of isiNdebele and chiShona languages commonly spoken in Zimbabwe, both meaning the rabbit. This nickname was derived from this nonsensical two-line rhyme I used to act out. The whole rhyme goes:

Parafina, parafina, nginathe ngaphi? (Parafin, Parafin, where should I drink?)

Mvundla-Tsuro. (Hare—Rabbit)

I am not sure where the fascination about my performance came about. With only two lines, there wasn't much to go with. I had to exaggerate my hand movements and move my head to the left and then right for the M*vundla-Tsuro* part. For some reason, my audience seemed to enjoy the actions. I remember the day I earned this name. My cousin Anna was visiting us at Ross Camp. I had been playing with my friends Francesca, Addlight, and Sylvia (for some reason, we called her Slivia) when I was called back home. I got home, and there was talk about me and this rhyme. Having heard so much about my performance, cousin Anna asked that I perform for her. I obliged and performed for her. All I remember is that I was being called by the nickname *"Mvundla-Tsuro,"* and for what? I do not know.

I was also called by the names of my favorite dolls I had acquired over the course of my short life. Such dolls' names included Kristabel, Lilibel, and Fisholo, just to name a few. I was called NaKristabel (mother of Kristabel) NaLilibel (mother of Lilibel) and NaFisholo (mother of Fisholo). I was also called *NaMbhobho* (Mother of a gun-shaped drink), a name derived from my favorite drink that came in the shape of a gun. The honor to bestow this nickname to me was given to the storekeeper Ndiweni. He was also given the honor to accept the money that had accidentally made it into my mouth and deliberately out through my rear end, thanks to my wild sister. Full story ahead.

Instead of spending our time locked up at Ross Camp, we would visit the suburbs where Black people lived. We were constant visitors to Makokoba, the oldest suburb for Black people, for various reasons. Haircuts were one of them. My hair type is the kind that is naturally full, coarse, kinky, and curly. It is beautiful but combing it is always a challenge. It can be combed and styled when wet. Once dry, it curls and looks like it has never known a comb. That is one reason I always visited a barber. My dad would decide to give his barber an early Christmas present by sending his whole family for the haircuts. I could not understand the sound of that thing called an electric shaving machine. It would be so loud it would sound like an airplane had landed on my head! What made it worse was when the barber would cut corners, he would hold my ear down and reach out on the soft spot behind my ears. I would jump in anticipation of a sliced ear each time the sound of that thing changed gear.

I was always afraid of having my ear cut off. The neck was even worse. The barber would move his shaving machine down to my neck! I don't think there were any hairs down there. He was just an evil man, together with his shaving machine. I am sure given a chance, that man would have moved that machine down my face as I saw him doing to my dad. I would wince, jump, scream, and cry so hard, but no one would come to my rescue. After the haircut, I would be completely exhausted. I knew I had to come up with a plan. To stop this madness, I planned a great performance during my next haircut. Since I had many tears and was a very good actress, this was not going to be a problem.

The next haircut found me ready! I was not going to mess around. My dad was going to see another side of me that he had never seen before! Was he going to arrest me? No. I sat on that evil highchair with my feet dangling in the air. My dad's barber smiled and greeted me cheerfully with my other known nickname, *"Mahlakanipheni."* He covered my chest with his white apron. His eyes were dancing mischievously. I noted that and challenged him to a "Bring it on barber, and you too, Mr. Policeman. This madness must stop, and it stops today!" I said this in my mind as I sat uncomfortably on that evil highchair. My dad smiled at me and reached out to take my hand to assure me. He opened my tight fist and placed what looked like candy (a sweet) in my hand.

This man was a genius! It is no wonder he had risen through the police ranks. I could not believe my eyes! My dad, in his infinite wisdom, had figured out the best plan in the world. My planned stunt of biting that evil barber disintegrated into thin air. What could be better than candy, a lollipop? Nothing could beat that. So, each time I visited that barber guy, I was rewarded with candy (sweets) before, during, and after the haircut, if I lived to tell. So, I endured the wrath of that barber and his evil shaving machine in exchange for my favorite treat. Problem solved. Maybe...

I am a December girl, and it takes the whole year for me to come of age compared to most of my friends. I used to envy my family and friends as they celebrated their birthdays earlier in the year, while I would have had to wait until the end of the year. As I got older, I liked this idea as it delayed my coming of age. A blessing in disguise. Soon after turning five years old, I was enrolled at Shaka Preschool. This was a prestigious preschool at the time, with Mrs. Sejo Mkandla as my teacher. As far as I was concerned, she was the best teacher in the whole wide world. Since I could not pronounce her name Mkandla, I resorted to "Nkandla." It was easy to pronounce since it rhymed with my clan's name Nkala. I loved this preschool and the teacher.

As much as I loved my preschool, there was one problem, however. That problem was causing me to think of dropping out of preschool. I did not know how to solve it. Bhibhi (Barnabas or B.B. for his initials), the campus ground technician, was my problem. I would find him cleaning the grounds, picking up leaves or figs in the morning, planting or watering the flowers. He would be welcoming children whose parents would bring them earlier, before Mrs. Nkandla's arrival. Everyone loved and respected him, and I did, too. He would give us figs if there were any and send us to the playground while waiting for Mrs. Nkandla. He took care of children whose parents were mostly police officers. I am not sure how my family's schedule worked, but dad was the one who took me to preschool. My dad would leave me in Bhibhi's care with other children. Each time Bhibhi would greet me cheerfully and say,

"How are you, *ntombi yami*?" (How are you, my girl?)

I would keep quiet in annoyance. His calling me his girl annoyed me to no end. There are three meanings to this type of address in my isiNdebele language. The address could simply mean one's daughter. Obviously, I was not his daughter. This could also be used as an endearing address by adults responsible for a young girl to show their love and appreciation for them. This address is the epitome of the African culture of raising a child in a village. Well, that is not what I thought Barnabas might have had in mind; I was sure of it. This address could also mean "girlfriend." This meaning is the one with which I charged Bhibhi. I assumed Bhibhi meant that I was his girlfriend. Young as I was, I knew what the word *"ntombi yami"* could mean. I lived with my brothers and uncles, and they had used that phrase constantly. My mother and aunties called me *"ntombi yami."* I knew what the phrase could mean and did not like it being used by Bhibhi in reference to me. I had had enough of this "my girl" nonsense. I was not going to have it any other day. I had to plan.

Since I always suffered from tonsillitis, thanks to a gene passed on through my maternal side of the family, my plan was going to be easily executed. One day, I refused to get out of bed and feigned sickness. This was going to be a problem because we did not have a babysitter at the time, and it was going to throw everyone's schedule into disarray. Too bad. Blame my mom's gene of tonsillitis. My older sibling reported my situation to my parents. Uncle Amon, who lived with us, had been my babysitter before deciding to train as a police officer. That checked him off the list of available babysitters. All my siblings were in school, and Mom was working. Dad could not just randomly take a day off.

Mom and dad had this habit of checking my temperature by putting the back of their hands on my forehead. Mom approached me and put her right hand on my forehead but could not feel the heat that she would normally feel when I had a temperature. She looked at me and wondered. Knowing how sick her children could get due to this curse of tonsillitis, she decided not to judge me. Her head was spinning, trying to figure out the schedule. Who would miss work or school to stay with her daughter? This was the million-dollar question. Just then, my uncle Amon came home from his night duty with nothing in his mind but a good day's sleep. Lo and behold, he had to rescue my mom from her dilemma. He had a night duty that day, so he grudgingly volunteered to stay with me. The problem, however, was that he wanted to sleep so he could be ready for work later that night. This meant that I was not going to be cared for until later, when the first brood of residents came home. I was content with that. Rather starve than hear that "my girl" nonsense.

As soon as my family was out, I also got out of bed and made myself comfortable in my home. Uncle Amon made some breakfast for me and went straight to his dreamland. I waited until I was sure he was deep in sleep before I made my move. Short as I was, I could not reach for the door handle. So, I put a chair by the door and used our coal stove hook to open the door. Swish, I was out. I knew Ross Camp like the back of my hand. Most of my age mates were not in school yet, not even in preschool. Most of them went straight to first grade without having gone through preschool. Formal education started in first grade. I was one of the few to start with preschool. I knew who would be available to play with and headed straight there. Put yourself in Uncle Amon's shoes when he woke up to find his "sick" niece missing and the door open. Since I had used a hook to open the door, I could not reach the door from outside to close it. The hook had been left hanging on the inside.

Not knowing the time, since I did not have a watch, and even if I had one, I could not tell time, I decided to go home before the brood came home. To my surprise, I found mom and all her children and Uncle Amon there. I was greeted cheerfully, but no one asked how I was. This was troubling. I'm not sure what my dearest Uncle Amon had told them. Everyone was looking at me with tantalizing eyes as if to laugh but holding back.

My family had inherited a laughing gene from my father, and woe to you if you were on the other side of the story. All the stories that were running through my head disappeared. I had hoped to get home early enough to continue with my acting career. Unfortunately, I had been delayed by the never-ending fun with best friends Sylvia, Francesca, and Addlight. Francesca's mother had delivered a new baby girl, which was fascinating to me. She had let us hold the little thing while she was doing some chores, and the little thing would wiggle and make funny noises and continue to sleep. She was a live version of my doll, Kristabel. That was fun. Time just rolled by, and before long, my stomach was growling, an indication that I needed to leave.

Since I was not allowed to eat anywhere except at home, I had to head home. We had spent a significant amount of time babysitting that adorable baby. My uncle did not have to worry about my whereabouts. He knew exactly where I was even without my telling him. He just did not bother bringing me back home. This was Ross Camp. No one could disappear without a trace at Ross Camp. Everyone was always accounted for. He was a cop, by the way. Little did I know that he was going to sell me out. Traitor!

"Dad will be off tomorrow so he can take you to the clinic for those tonsils. An injection will help a lot."

That was my mom. I froze. She knew I was not sick. How she knew baffled me. How can she know so much! My mom was a behavioral psychologist. She knew exactly how scared I was of an injection or a shot. I feared that thing and Nurse Nsingo, who worked at the clinic.

Nurse Nsingo was the worst nurse in the world. She would tell you to lie on your stomach so she could inject that needle into your bottom (buttock/behind). I would tighten my bottom to stop the pain from paralyzing me. She would move up my dress and find her target. She would clean the targeted spot. She would prepare her weapon, and I would relax momentarily, thinking that she was still preparing it. Before I knew it, that weapon would be deep in my small bottom. She would jab my bottom with an intent to cause grievous bodily harm. The pain would be excruciating. One shot, and the tonsils would bid me farewell. Unfortunately, most of the times, five shots were prescribed. By the end of the five shots, my bottom would be so painful I would not even be able to sit. No, I was not going to get a shot from Nurse Nsingo for no apparent reason. I had to decide what was better, an injection or the "my girl" nonsense. I had to come up with a plan.

"I feel better now. There will be no need to go to the

clinic," I responded to my mom, wondering what my next step would be.

I felt dejected. Nothing was working well. My acting career had started on a good note but came crumbling before my eyes. My very best friend, my Uncle Amon, had betrayed me. And my psychologist mom could read my brain like lightning and outsmart me with every move.

I was not going to tell anyone the real reason for my missing preschool. No one in this house could solve my dilemma. Only one person could. My hero. And he alone I was going to tell. He came home from work, and as usual, I was sitting on his lap. He was the only one who asked how I was feeling. I told him the truth. He smiled but did not judge me. He understood. And no, he had not taken a day off to take me to the clinic to meet the wrath of Nurse Nsingo. My mom had made that up. That psychologist of a mother always had tricks up her sleeves!

The following day I was up and ready. My hero walked me to preschool as usual. The preschool dropout was back to school, looking as healthy and confident as ever! I still remember the conversation between my dad and the ground technician.

"Yah, Bhanabhasi." (Hi, Barnabas). My hero had ap-

proached Bhibhi and greeted him as usual.

"Linjani, mdala?" (How are you, sir?) echoed Bhibhi.

Bhibhi's face had lit up, and his white teeth had luminated his sunburned dark skin. He had smiled affectionately at my hero and me while putting the figs in the can. He had proceeded to clean his hands on his apron to shake my hero's hand.

"My daughter tells me you call her your wife."

Bhibhi's smile had faded as quickly as it had emerged. He froze as he met my hero's threatening stare. Without waiting for Bhibhi's response, my hero had continued,

"Please do not ever say that again because she does not like being called your wife. I may have to arrest you if you continue saying that to her. She missed school yesterday because of that."

My hero, in his police uniform, stood towering over Bhibhi, the ground technician, with his little angel confidently standing by his side. My hero commanded respect. He was not going to have his little angel miss school because of some goofy guy. Mr. Policeman had to straighten up this goofy guy. He had threatened to arrest him! Ahh, that was fun! There I was, ever so proud of this man called my father, my defender, my hero, Mr. Policeman!

"I am sorry, Captain." Bhibhi looked puzzled. "I have never called *uMahlakanipheni* my wife. I've called her my girl...Oh! I see!" Just then, Bhibhi got an epiphany! "I'm sorry, Captain. I will not call her my girl ever again. I apologize sincerely." My dad and Bhibhi locked their gaze, and both nodded at the same time. That was the end of that "my girl" nonsense, and I continued enjoying my preschool year. Bhibhi, who was of Malawian descent, learned an isiNdebele lesson that day.

This incident, while it may have been innocent to Bhibhi, for me, it was detestable to the extent that I was prepared to drop out of preschool. Having thought of all possible meanings of the phrase *"ntombi yami"* at my age, I was able to determine what I thought Bhibhi meant. I had used avoidance as a way of coping with my problem. By dropping out of preschool, I had thought I would solve the problem. When that did not work out, I had to find another solution. I revered my father, and nothing could happen to me under his watch. He was dependable and a pillar I could lean on. This situation defined me as a child, and I was grateful to have a father like mine.

I loved singing. One of the songs we used to sing

showed our love for our teacher, Mrs. Nkandla. It went as follows:

"Wozani nonke, (Come all)

Sithandazele umistress weth' uNkandla, (so we could pray for our teacher Mrs. Nkandla)

Siyamthanda, uyasithanda." (We love her, she loves us).

We would combine this love song with another one showing how we loved each other like children who were in Mrs. Nkandla's class. This one went as follows:

"Masibambaneni (Let us hold each other's hand)

Thina sobabili (the two of us)

Thin' esifundayo (who go to school)

Esithand' amatitshala. (who love our teachers).

Ngifak' unyawo lwami, (I put my foot forward),

Ngikhiph' unyawo lwami, (and I remove my foot),

Ngilunyikinyise, besengiphenduka." (and shake it, shake it, then turn around).

For this song, we would hold hands, and I would be lifting other children's hands high enough for Mrs. Nkandla to see. I would be putting my foot forward, giving it a good shaking, and then turning around. It is no surprise that I fell several times while performing this part of the song. I just loved the song. I enjoyed music and movement, and Mrs. Nkandla tapped into that.

Besides my best teacher Mrs. Nkandla, I also loved reciting nursery rhymes and acting them out too. For some reason, I would stand out in a group either singing out loud, exaggerating with my hands when other children were keeping their hands to self, or laughing my heart out. I would hear people commenting after a performance that I did a great job. I would wonder why my acting was considered outstanding. Why would a person not act out a song when it had action words? Why not belch it out when a song demanded that? Think about the Jack and Jill rhyme that follows:

Jack and Jill went up the hill

To get a tin of water.

Jack fell down and broke his crown

And Jill came tumbling after.

This rhyme is action-packed and deserves to be acted out. I would visualize this song in my head and see how it could be acted out. Although English was my second language, Mrs. Nkandla had explained what the rhyme meant, and I found it interesting.

One day, our teacher Mrs. Nkandla told us we were going on an excursion to the Khami Ruins on the outskirts of Bulawayo. We were going to prepare individual and group presentations to entertain our families and the invited guests. One of our group presentations was the *Jack and Jill* rhyme. I loved that rhyme. It was action-packed, and I was looking forward to the actions. Ideas flooded my head.

What about if I pushed down that boy called Ndaba so he could fall down and break his crown, and I would come tumbling after him? Hmmm. Brilliant! I thought to myself.

I planned this action secretly for weeks once Mrs. Nkandla confirmed our presentations. Ndaba was the perfect candidate for this performance for several reasons. He was my friend. We both lived at Ross Camp since his father was a police officer like mine. His father was also the headmaster/principal at Ross Camp primary, where we were both going to enroll for our first grade. I had heard that Ndaba's father was trouble, though, and was feared by the whole school. I am not sure if I was looking forward to that. Anyway, I was going to act this beautiful rhyme with his son.

Acting with Ndaba would be fun, I thought. As my friend, he sometimes helped push me on the swing during our recess. He knew his colors and numbers just like me, and we both always seemed to answer questions thrown at us by Mrs. Nkandla. Ndaba was also a brave boy because he could drink his skimmed milk in a gulp. I could never drink that thing; it tasted like paint. Why in the world would anyone make children drink that paint or whitewash? Why we were not given regular milk mystified me. For that, I respected Ndaba.

We prepared individual performances and group performances. Obviously, my individual performance was going to be action-packed!

On the day of the excursion, my mom, a fashionista, dressed me in my best outfit—my gym dress. This was a red and white plaid strap dress just up to my knees. It was worn with a white long-sleeved shirt, white shoes, and white ankle socks. I looked very expensive in it and felt it too. With a bald head, I felt confident and intelligent.

Mom and me on the day of the excursion.

For the class performance of the nursery rhyme, I was going to knock the ball out of the park by knocking down my friend Ndaba so he could break his crown, and I would come tumbling after. I was not sure if Ndaba would think about acting this song the way I did. I just wanted to use him to demonstrate the rhyme. He was not going to mind, I thought. I needed to take action to make sure the nursery rhyme got the attention it deserved. Mrs. Nkandla had not thought of giving us tins or cans so we could get some water, as the rhyme suggested. She must have read my mind because I would have asked her to put some water in it too, so I could do justice to the most deserving nursery rhyme. Ah, well, that was fine. I was sure she had forgotten. I was going to make this a memorable performance anyway, with or without tins or cans of water.

We all stood up and lined in our positions as per instruction. I had positioned myself close to Ndaba so I could use him as my prop. So, as we got to the part when Jack "fell down," I hooked my arm right under Ndaba's in preparation for the act. I was about to push him when I looked down and saw his mother smiling at me. Oh, no! I quickly let go of Ndaba. Just then, I had an epiphany. If I went ahead with the plan, I would mess up my beautiful gym dress, my white shirt, and white ankle socks. The ground Ndaba was going to fall on was dusty. This performance would have cost me more than I would have bargained for. It was too risky. I abandoned all the weeks of my acting career right there and then.

Seeing Ndaba's mother smiling at me or at us sent waves of confusion to my five-year-old mind. Did she know I wanted to push her son? Wait a minute... did she think... oh, no, no, no!

My sister Nhlanhla had taught me a song in our isiN-
debele (IsiZulu) language about a guy named George who
had a hunting gun and would shoot with it. But while hunting, he peeked from his hunting gun and saw a small bird
that kept skipping about. He tried to catch it, but he got
choked by some smoke. The isiNdebele/isiZulu song went:

*"UGeorge uyadubula nxa elombhobho x 2 (George
shoots when he has a gun)*

*Wabelunguza kancane, wabelunguza kancane, (He
kept peeking)*

*Wabon' inyon' encane iyaqayeqayo. (And he saw a
small bird skipping about)*

*Wath' uyayibamba, wath' uyayibamba (He tried
catching it)*

*Wahitshwa yintuthu. (He got choked by some
smoke)*

Oho! Oho!

Wahitshwa yintuthu (He got choked by some smoke)

Oho!

*Wahitshwa yintuthu." (He got choked by some
smoke).*

Imagine the actions in this song! So many verbs, adjectives, and onomatopoeia. First, it is George holding a gun and peering through its hole. Then, he sees a small bird hopping and skipping about. He tries to catch the small bird, but he gets choked by some smoke. I took the song to another level and owned it. At my age, I had an angelic voice that needed no training. I was unaware of it myself, but many people would comment about it, hence the constant plea for me to sing. It took me years to figure that out. And as the youngest of six children, I made no contribution at home. Everyone had to take care of me, which was a chore. So, the one place I could be heard and noticed was at school or with my friends.

Back to the song. To demonstrate the first part of the George song, my sister had given me a stick that acted as a gun. I was shooting everyone, including my classmates behind me and on my sides and the families who were spectators. I could have easily poked some eyes if they had not ducked. I was not shooting them because I had a vendetta; I was shooting because I was demonstrating. It was war! Imagine the scene! I am a five-year-old girl with some missing teeth and a couple of gaps, I am dressed in my best outfit, a gym dress, and I am carrying a "gun." My dad, Mr. Policeman, is right there with other families as a spectator! It was a great performance.

The next part was the peering one through a hole. I held my "gun" closely, the way I imagined my dad would, and stood at attention like a police officer. I had seen my dad at their parade or training, so I knew how they held their guns. I lifted my right hand and cupped it over my forehead as if sheltering myself from the sun and then peeked through it. I could see my dad and many others in stitches, and as if to say, "This is for you, Mr. Policeman," I lowered my voice and sang in a staccato to emphasize the peeping.

Now comes my favorite part, the part when George tries to catch the bird but gets choked by some smoke. I put my "gun" down and raised my voice for the part about George's effort to catch the small bird. I raised my voice for this part to indicate George's confidence in catching the small bird. I clasped my hands to show an attempt to catch the bird and coughed the "Oho!" part to indicate George's choking. I am not sure why this performance sent everyone in stitches. I could see them tearing. As for my dear Mr. Policeman, his laughing-out-loud gene had been triggered by his little angel actress, and there was no stopping this machine gun. He had to move out of his seat to stop himself from laughing. That performance defined me. It lingered on my mind so vividly for the longest time, and I was the talk of my family and neighborhood for as long as I could remember.

This is Shaka Preschool, where it all began.

Yes, I could unleash my creativity in many ways. I was a little actress.

Chapter 3

The Brood

As my family navigated through the Zimbabwe War of Liberation, it is important to understand their personality and the impact each member had in my life. As a close-knit family, each member's contribution in my life was invaluable. Each of my siblings contributed to shaping my life, intentionally or unintentionally. Since I was the youngest, they each would be tasked or would feel the need to care for me. In some cases, I am not sure what the motivation was for taking such a responsibility when both my parents were alive. I guess they could not help it. As my father's brood, we inherited one of his obvious traits—his laughing gene. Humor was part of us, and we were constantly laughing. There are many memorable stories that we shared as a family that qualified into our Laughing Gene's Book of Records.

Emmanuel was my mother's firstborn and my older brother. If I were to list positive characteristics, he was the kind who could check them all off. In my mind, he was the perfect brother. He was intelligent, kind, humorous, and mischievous. He knew his arithmetic very well. He could add and subtract in a heartbeat and would use his arithmetic skills to his benefit. Not always did we have enough treats for all six of us. Many times, we had to share among ourselves. My brother, being the eldest and the most intelligent, would figure out the math problem while the younger brood looked in awe. For instance, if we were to share four oranges among the six of us, he would give each an orange so that he and my older sister would be the ones without an orange. He would emphasize that the two of them were the only ones without an orange, appealing to us to share with them. He would then ask each of us to cut the orange in half to share with them. He would give my older sister her half, and he would get the rest. Yes, he would get the rest. If you do the calculations, you know how many oranges he ended up enjoying. That was brilliant! I did not figure out this math problem until years later, when he confessed. I was stunned.

With his ingenuity, my big brother could do almost anything he set his mind on. To keep us entertained, he would create a story or a song based on our family events. The songs and stories would be so impactful and would linger in my mind forever. Since there were only two bedrooms and a lounge, our sleeping arrangements were sometimes a challenge. The girls used the second bedroom, and the boys used the lounge. Boys sometimes found themselves having to sleep in the kitchen if we were visited by a married couple. Girls would move to the lounge and offer our bedroom to the couple. As girls, we shared a queen bed among the four of us. Yes, among the four of us. We had figured out a creative way to make this work. Two girls would face the upper part of the bed while the other two girls would face the lower part. Creative as the plan appeared, it did not always work out well.

As the youngest and the shortest, I would wake up with someone's foot in my mouth. I eventually learned to bite whatever was on and/or in my mouth. We would have someone falling off the bed and taking with her all the blankets. Sometimes I would wake up with a cramped leg or arm due to limited space to change positions. I would have someone purposely passing gas, knowing well that the gas would be heading in my direction. I do not know how often I got choked up. I would throw the blankets away to expose the culprit's feet.

One day I decided to report the passing gas saga to the crown prince, my big brother himself. I did not know what action he was going to take, but I trusted he would intervene in the most memorable fashion known in the books. And indeed, he did. He did not disappoint. He delivered! He composed a song as a rebuke to his young sisters for the unacceptable behavior. Besides its interesting tune, one reason this song was impactful was that we found it funny for someone to even think of composing a song based on passing gas. It was novel. My siblings and I laughed at this song for a long time.

Since my brother Emmanuel was older, he used to be tasked with cutting or shaving my hair if Dad did not have enough money to take us to the barber's shop. At the time, my family did not have a shaving machine, only a pair of scissors. I was afraid of haircuts and scissors. I would wince and twirl with each cut, and that would lead to my brother making my hair uneven *(amatheza),* whether purposely or accidentally, that I have never been able to determine. After the uneven haircut, I would look like a puppet!

My hairstyle, or lack of thereof, would send the whole family in stitches and tears for a week. The whole neighborhood would be in stitches, too. Some would try to hide their laughing faces, but others would find it impossible to hold their laughter, and they would laugh out loud to fulfill my brother's wish. I would be subjected to weeks of comic relief until my hair grew and evened out. Luckily, my hair always grew back fast, which was also a problem since it meant more visits to a barber. My saving grace in some instances was my ever-so-near tears that I would use as a weapon. I later learned to join in the fun and enjoy the uneven hairstyle. Why not?

Now comes the worst part. For other haircut appointments with my barber brother, I had to choose between the uneven cut or the smooth one. Given my experience regarding the uneven cut, I would opt for the clean shave. Armed with a pair of scissors, my brother would start the process and chop all the hair off. He would then move with precision to even out the hair. The final process would be to smooth out even behind the ear. This is the part when barber brother would press the pair of scissors on my head, as was recommended, to get rid of all the hair. In the process, sometimes, my barber brother would "accidentally" snip off my skin. I would squeal and squeak while holding my ear. The end of this hair-cutting ordeal was always welcome.

After enduring what I considered a gruesome hair-cutting and ear-snipping ordeal, barber brother would pat my clean-shaven head and introduce her bald and beautiful little sister to the onlookers. He had this ridiculous claim that patting one's head after a shave helped one's hair grow and was an acceptable tip for the barber. How and why I believed it, beats me. He would laugh so hard tears would roll down his cheeks. I would hear his laughter from the house. That laughing gene!

My brother Emmanuel's creative mind also led him to create a never-ending story about a character he named Georgy Mganu, based on his family characters. We all suspected that the main character Georgy Mganu was him because he was the hero in the story. To make the story even more interesting, big brother composed a nonsensical song to go along with the story. When growing up, there was this habit or culture where young children would ask or have an adult eat their corn/maize cob first to "open the way" for them. While being tasked with "opening a way" for me, big brother would eat half my corn/maize instead of eating the first line, as was the custom. It was during one of these maize-way-opening practices that he composed one of the songs that became dear to us as a family.

"Sasihamba eGoli (We were going to eGoli (Johannesburg).)

Sidl' umumbu (Eating corn/maize)

Sahamba, sahamba, sahamba (We walked, walked, and walked.)

Sidl' umumbu sahamba. (Eating corn/maize)

Tiri tiri diti riti didiri-di (sound of a lead guitar)

Ditiri ditiri tididiri-di." (sound of a lead guitar)

When singing this song, big brother would stand and dance while pretending to play guitar. He would bend and move his legs back and forth. He would take a step forward and backward carefully, as if afraid of stepping on dirt. The brood and cousin Tsatsi would follow behind him, singing in harmony and dancing along. The song was beautifully composed, and we enjoyed it so much.

Orpha, the second-born and first girl, was always the responsible one. She was like a mother figure; we all relied on her. She was confident, intelligent, and creative. Her creative mind propelled her to do anything that she set her mind to do. She was the best cook in the world. No doubt, she had learned her cooking skills from the best, our mother. She would turn a simple recipe into a mouth-watering delicious meal. She was also armed with a ferocious dressmaking skill! She would turn a simple dress into a runway display.

Besides her skills, Orpha was a beautiful soul, both inside and out. Armed with my father's inherited diastema, *itsako*, a gap between upper two front teeth, her smile would dazzle the beholder. Her infectious smile, oozing from her pure heart, would light up even the heartless. This deep processor, who was also a natural leader, was the most revered in the family.

I came home one day to see my big sister Orpha inject herself on her thigh. I screamed as I was reminded of Nurse Nsingo's injection on my small behind. Yes, my sister Orpha had been diagnosed with type 1 diabetes at sixteen years of age. Her blood sugar levels would constantly drop, and she would go into a comma. Her illness caused so much heartache. We could see how depressed my mother became after the diagnosis and how hard she tried to be strong. We all rallied around my sister and provided the support she needed. Even at my age, I also learned to tell when she needed sugar or candy (sweets) to boost her sugar levels and how to make the sugar solution to give her during her episodes. Her syringes were sterilized by boiling. There were no medical advances at the time. Several times she was in a coma and admitted to the hospital.

Shepherd was the third born and the younger of the

two boys. He, too, had inherited my father's laugh-out-loud gene. He had a good sense of humor and was a good storyteller. He would tell a story and use simple, colorful language that would leave one in stitches. If one was telling a story, he would be adding phrases as if he had witnessed the situation. That would make the story even juicier. Like my sister Orpha, he too had inherited my father's *itsako* (diastema).

I do not forget one day when my brother Shepherd almost got me killed by his friend, Cephas. But it did not work. Cephas came home looking for my brother Shepherd; unfortunately, my brother was not home that day. Cephas found me standing by the door, just about to get in the house. Since my brother was not home at that time, I promised to let him know of his friend's visit. When Shepherd came home, I told him about his friend Cephas's visit and that he had given me fertilizer. My brother was puzzled and concerned about why his friend would give me fertilizer. When asked what I had done with the fertilizer, I told my brother that I had eaten it.

Being a concerned brother, Shepherd reported the incident to my mother. My family was thrown into confusion and panic, wondering why my brother's friend would feed me fertilizer. My mother panicked and started giving me some milk to drink so it could dilute the poison or at least cause me to vomit or pass it out. My brother had to run like a mad man to look for his friend to verify this information. Luckily, he found him as soon as he had left. Cephas was also on his way home to look for my brother Shepherd again. Cephas confirmed he had given me sherbet, not fertilizer. Sherbet is a powder made with real fruit flavor eaten as a sweet or used to make a drink, especially for children. I loved sherbet. I survived that day. Those big words must have confused me. Fertilizer. Sherbet. What's the difference? Who cares? They are both powders. And what was up with all that panic! Adults!

The story of the fertilizer and sherbet earned a place in my family's Laughing Gene's Book of Records. One would guess I was the laughingstock. No. When the course was clear, and everyone was assured I had eaten sherbet, not fertilizer, the laughter was beyond imaginable. It was hysterical. Uncle Amon would even imitate my small voice on how I had reported having eaten fertilizer. Since there were many characters involved in this story, the shift turned from me to include Her Highness, my mother first, for panicking and making me drink milk with the hope that I would puke the fertilizer, to Shepherd, whose reaction was priceless after hearing I had eaten fertilizer. He had run like a madman to look for Cephas and determine what he had given me to eat. Attention was also turned to Uncle Amon, who had had the responsibility of babysitting me.

We could not laugh at mom in her presence; that would be insensitive. She had many responsibilities, a lot to deal with. We could not laugh at her in her presence. Laughing behind her back gave us more pleasure than could be described. Ahh, the power of forbidden laughter!

Nhlanhla was the quiet and calm one. Her name means luck or fortune. My father gave her this name because they considered themselves fortunate to have had a girl after having a boy first, a girl, another boy, and then a girl. There seemed to be a lucky draw to their lineup. She was the most beautiful in our family, both inside and out. She, too, had inherited my father's diastema, *itsako*, a gap between upper two front teeth. Hers was as big as my father's. When she smiled, and that gap was revealed, her dazzling beauty radiated and illuminated the sky.

With her wasp waist, she was envied by many of her peers. She was commonly known as *ilamba lidlile* (one who eats but still maintains a small waist and looks like she is hungry). She earned this nickname because she maintained a small waistline. Her big eyes, adorned with long natural lashes, spoke. They spoke humor, they spoke pain, they spoke love. One could not help but be captivated by her exquisite beauty.

My sister Nhlanhla could sing too. Her angelic voice would transport one's soul to heavenly glory. She taught me a song I sang for my individual performance for our excursion at preschool. That song, combined with my acting, defined me.

From left to right: Nhlanhla, me, Mom, and Thando.

Due to our being two years apart in age, my sister Thando was the closest, the wildest, and the most influential of the brood in my life. Her name, Thando, means love. Being one of the most talkative in the family, she would keep the family entertained. Also armed with a signature *itsako* (diastema), her dazzling smile would illuminate the sky and show off her gap. Her hearty contagious laughter would resonate, and I would find myself laughing uncontrollably.

Thando was an intelligent and creative girl. Her creative mind always drove her to do the craziest things one would imagine. I am the only one in my family who cannot ride a bike. This is because, at the age of eight years, my sister had learned to ride a bike, the adult one with a crossbar. She decided to give me a ride, and I obliged. I was six years old at the time. I remember her riding down the street with me seated behind her, and the next thing, we were both down. From that time, I feared riding a bike. Unfortunately, we did not have tricycles, so I could progress easily from three wheels to two. Her Highness, the Honorable Judge Mother, presided over the case and barred my sister from ever giving me a bike ride. Well, I took this to another level and decided not to ride a bike ever in my life!

Since Thando and I were close in age, we spent most of our time together. She would come up with the most ridiculous stories and the craziest solutions for my problems. Among many stories or events we shared, I never forget the solution to one of my problems.

I loved candies/sweets, particularly suckers/lollipops. So, I always had pocket money in the sum of no more than five cents. One of the coins at the time was *itiki* (two and a half cents). That day I did not have a pocket to put my money in. So, I decided to put it in my mouth while swinging on the swing before class. I accidentally swallowed the *itiki* coin. My sister had emphatically warned me of three things not to swallow. Yes, three things. One: a needle. Two: a razor blade. Three: a coin. I do not even know why one would swallow these items anyway. She had told me that swallowing these items would cause death.

After swallowing my *itiki* pocket money, I thought I was going to die. I was miserable in class that day, wondering when I was going to die or whether I was dead already. I kept wondering how dead people behaved, so Mrs. Nkandla could see that I was dead and let my family know. That day, Mrs. Nkandla wondered what was wrong with me. She probably had an easier class that day. I hardly raised my hand to answer questions that day, nor did I compete for Mrs. Nkandla's attention. Normally if she asked a question that most of us knew, we would shoot up our hands or sometimes even stand on our tippy toes with hands in the air while calling her name. She would pick one person to answer the question. Sometimes I would be disappointed at not having been picked to answer the question. At times, I did not care. On this day, since I was either dead or dying, I did not care to answer those questions. I kept wondering when I was going to die, that is, if I was not dead yet. I did enjoy my soup, though, eating it as a dead or dying person. I talked with a hoarse voice as I thought that was how dead people talked.

After school, my sister was waiting for me on the other side of the busy street because I had learned to cross the street by myself. I was only five years old at that time. So, I crossed the street to meet my sister. Instead of heading straight to the grocery store, as usual, we headed home first. I had told her what had happened to my money. She made the diagnosis there and then. She comforted me and told me not to worry; I was not going to die because she had a solution. My fearless and wild sister! Always a step ahead!

We went home, and she told me to let her know when it was time to empty my bowels. It did not take long before duty called. I told my sister, and we made a beeline for the bathroom/toilet. She was prepared. She had all the necessary equipment for the procedure. Once in the bathroom/toilet, she laid a paper on the floor, and I emptied my bowels on it. With precision, she used her forceps (in the form of a stick) to locate the missing coin. Since it was silver, it was easy to identify. My brilliant sister had removed the valuable coin from my poop.

She cleaned the coin somehow, but how she did it should be left to anyone's imagination. Whether she cleaned the mess on the bathroom floor or not is a conversation for another day. The point is that I had swallowed a coin and lived to tell, and with the help of my wild sister, I recovered what had belonged to me. The next thing I knew, I was at the grocery store where I bought my lucky packet (candy packet with a toy inside) and my favorite drink in the form of a gun.

"Yebo, NaMbhobho!" (Hello, Mother of the Gun-shaped drink!) The storekeeper, Mr. Ndiweni, had gleefully greeted me.

He had taken the honor to bestow upon me this nickname, *NaMbhobho,* based on my liking of this drink called *umbhobho* (the gun) because it came in a gun-shaped plastic container. After exchanging greetings, he accepted my infamous *itiki* (two and a half cents, which was the size of an American dime) in exchange for my favorite drink, *umbhobho,* the gun-shaped drink. Yes, whereas I was dead, I was now alive! Thanks to my wild sister.

There is one story that my sister told me, which was clearly out of her imagination. Since I believed everything that she told me, I could not differentiate between her imagination and reality. Her imagination had led her to tell me a story about her fourth-grade classmate, Aziko. We had laughed for several days nonstop.

At Ross Camp Primary School, we were required to attend school assembly so we could be checked for cleanliness. We were supposed to have our hair cut short. Hence the constant haircuts and barbers I had to endure. Thando had started by laughing, a sure sign that she was my father's daughter. She narrated the story that she claimed to have heard about Aziko, their classmate. Aziko was the clown of the school.

Two days later, at assembly, I saw Aziko. Due to his height, he was towering above all students. I imagined him passing gas and excreting a boiled egg in the process and eating the egg. I just could not help it. I burst out with uncontrollable laughter. Those around me turned and looked at me with fear on their faces, knowing what Principal Ndlovu would do to me for disrupting the assembly. Some joined in laughter without even knowing what I was laughing at. It was hysterical. This was forbidden laughter. It is like when you are having a family prayer, and your guest who is tone-deaf starts a hymn completely out of tune. You are supposed to harmonize but do not know how and you do not even know whether to laugh or cry. Or when a family member tries to reach a Bible in the front pew and accidentally passes gas, looks around, praying that no one heard where the squeaky sound came from. If you have a laughing gene, laughing at church would be memorable. Ahh, the power of forbidden laughter!

I was exhausted from laughing. I could barely stand up. I woke up from my laughing stupor with tears running down my cheeks to see a pair of big black shiny shoes planted on the ground where I was standing. With teary eyes and a broken rib, I straightened up to meet and greet this gigantic monster, the Incredible Hulk, who was towering over me. I came face to face with none other than Principal Ndlovu, who also happened to be a police officer. This was my preschool friend, Ndaba's father. I do not know who I was in Mr. Principal's eyes- a foe or a future daughter-in-law.

With feet dangling from the hard bench in Mr. Principal's office, I crossed my hands on my chest to show humility. I took a quick glance at Mr. Principal and avoided his piercing gaze. In my culture, it is not permissible to look directly into an elder's eyes. Children who do that are considered rude and disrespectful. I made sure I presented a humble and apologetic demeanor. All I knew at that moment was that I was in big trouble. I was a good girl; I was never that person who wanted to be in trouble. All I had known was law and order, but that day my brain had not agreed with me.

Five children had been identified as having aided a criminal. The five children had also been called to the principal's office. They had to explain their unacceptable behavior before Mr. Principal. They failed to come up with a reasonable explanation. They had laughed simply because I was laughing. At this response, Mr. Principal looked puzzled and shifted his attention to me. He asked me to explain why I had laughed during assembly, knowing fully well that the rules required utter silence. I had been taught to tell the truth to a cop no matter what. I could lie to my family and friends but not to cops.

My dad would tell us ridiculous lies that people would tell to get out of infractions. We would laugh at those that lacked logic. I did not want to end up like them. For that reason, I had to tell Mr. Principal the reason for my laughing during assembly. I tried to find a more acceptable word for "excretion" than the course one that my sister had used. My brain worked fast, but I could not find a better word. The one word that came to mind was one used to describe babies when they are passing a stool. No, that would be ridiculous to use that word, given that Aziko was a big boy. I abandoned that thought.

I narrated my story and used the same coarse word that my sister had used to describe the Aziko incident. The problem with that word in my isiNdebele language is that it just sounds so heavy and vulgar. It is not a word that is thrown around like a ball. The other children were hearing the story for the first time. Two of them burst out with laughter while others struggled to control themselves. I could hear giggles and sniffles and could see bodies vibrating in laughter. Some hid their faces in their hands. Laughing is contagious. I am sure others were saying,

"I might as well have a good laugh; after all, I'm here

for punishment!"

Mr. Principal had not laughed. Neither had I. I had struggled to keep a straight face. I wanted to present a better me in the hope that my punishment would be less severe. Mr. Principal exhibited various facial expressions that I had found disturbing. At hearing the isiNdebele word that I had used for excretion, Mr. Principal had winced and curled his mouth. As I concluded the story, Mr. Principal had stared at me, raised his hawk-like eyebrows, twitched his mouth to his side, and twisted his long mustache. He looked dumbfounded as if he wanted to say,

"Wait...What? What on earth?"

After what seemed like an eternity to me, he sighed and shook his head. I wondered what his behavior meant. I could not accurately read adult facial language at the time. I waited for my sentence. I am sure his son Ndaba had told him numerous stories about me. I am sure he had wanted to laugh too. He knew my father. Why would he be surprised at my behavior? I am sure he was saying to himself,

"Oh, boy! The apple does not fall far from its tree!"

I am sure he was also regretting why he ever asked me the reason for my laughter. Some things are better left unknown.

For punishment, we had to clean the school ground that afternoon after school. This was my first time being engaged in hard labor. Picking up papers was hard labor. The only thing closest to hard labor I had ever done at the time was carrying my plate or dish to the sink for my sisters to clean or to have it filled with porridge for second servings. Mr. Principal was not playing. He was a law enforcer, and he meant business.

I refuse to take responsibility for this behavior. I blame my sister for telling me such a ridiculously juicy story. I blame Mr. Policeman, my father, for his laughing-out-loud gene. I could not help myself. Once that laughing trigger was pulled, there was no stopping.

I was only in first grade. I had a long way to go. With such experiences, there was no telling where I was headed.

Thando, Mom, and me behind our infamous toilet.

My family was an epitome of love and joy, a sturdy foundation for a future. Together, we would face challenges and dilemmas and find solutions where possible.

Chapter 4

My Hero

My father, Jonathan Jonah Maphosa (Jonah, as he was commonly known), was my hero. His physical characteristics and personality set him apart, making him a larger-than-life character whose presence and influence could not be ignored. He was a relatively tall man, towering at about six feet three inches (one point nine meters) in height. His slender, strong, and athletic physique was an indication that his physical health mattered to him.

There are sixteen official languages spoken in Zimbabwe, and the different cultures are acknowledged and celebrated as being Zimbabwean. As part of the amaNdebele cultural group, who speak isiNdebele language, my hero's cultural identity could not be mistaken. He had had his ear lobes slit, a process known in isiNdebele language as *ukuklekla*. It was believed at the time that this process was a way of raising a strong and fearless Ndebele nation and setting them apart. He would tell of this *ukukleka* process and what it meant for his culture. A normal-sized pen would fit into his ear holes. He took pride in his cultural identity.

My father had *itsako* (diastema), a big gap that separated his upper two teeth. This was a signature characteristic that four of his children, Orpha, Shepherd, Nhlanhla, and Thando, had inherited. This gap was large enough to fit the lower part of his tongue. His infectious smile and chuckle would reveal this signature gap and infect people around him with laughter. One could not help but be mesmerized by this larger-than-life character.

He kept his hair short and well-kempt, with *umqhekezo*, a semi-permanent line parting his hair in the middle. This parting line eventually became permanent. His constant visit to the barber would attest to the reason for the short hair. His mustache covered his upper lip, and he would at times twirl the beard so it looked like cat whiskers.

While his physical appearance set him apart, his character is what mattered and matters to me the most. His infectious smile and chuckle would reveal his exuberant personality. His signature wholesome, hearty laughter defined him as a joyful individual and would send other people joining in the laughter even without knowing the cause of the laughter. He would be seen or heard rolling with laughter, with tears running down his cheeks. As a great storyteller, he always kept his audience, friends, and family captivated. He was a cheerful man whose laughing gene and story-telling skill the family had inherited and enjoyed. Through him, I learned how laughter heals and uplifts one's soul.

From left to right: Aunt Jelitha, Nhlanhla, Dad, Thando, Mom, me, and Orpha.

My hero's presence in my life impacted my perspective and drove me to find strength within me when there seemed to be none. He oozed confidence and bravery. He was the kind that would defy a warning against visiting a certain area because it was dangerous or there was a lion lurking in the vicinity. He would be that guy who would say,

"No, that's rubbish. What danger? Do not be cowards."
And he would carefully plan and either attack the enemy
or find a way out.

He was a confident man, both in word and in deed.
He walked with confidence and talked with confidence. He
would encourage those who would have wanted to give up
on a difficult task. He would constantly say,

"Do not be overcome by a task. A task does not talk
back; it does not challenge you verbally. A task challenges
your brain and physique, that's all. Face it head-on!" He
would be heard in isiNdebele saying, *"Ungehlulwa yinto
engakhulumiyo."* (Do not be challenged by something that
does not talk).

We would take that to mean that every task should be
considered doable since tasks do not talk back. We lived
by those words, believing that tasks must be faced head-on
and dealt with since they were meant to challenge one's
physical and/or mental state. Those words molded me.

My hero's calm demeanor and confidence brought a
sense of security to me as his little girl. Nothing could happen to me or my family if he was there.

My hero was the eighth of ten siblings, with three boys

and seven girls. He was the youngest of the three boys. He was born in 1930 in the Mtshabezi-Wenlock area of Gwanda North in Zimbabwe. His mother, MaMoyo, had died when he was nine years old, leaving him in the care of his older seven siblings. His father, Grandpa Tshandiwana, had remarried after the death of his wife and had had four more sons, Mpande, James, Johanne, and Irvin.

The year my father was born, the then Rhodesian government enacted the Land Apportionment Act of 1930. This landmark act was the first attempt at legalizing the process of sharing land between Black and White people. The government established native purchase areas and made it illegal for Black people to buy land outside the designated areas. Although a minority, White people took most of the land, and Black people were left with small, designated land. Before the Land Apportionment Act (1930), land was not openly accessible to Black people, but there was no law to bar them from owning land (Jennings, 1935).

With the Land Apportionment Act also came the establishment of Native Reserves, *amarizeva*. White settlers (as they were known) were provided more land, which tended to consist of richer soil and higher rainfall. Black people were forced to relinquish their land and were given land in dry areas where farming was difficult. My father's family was removed from the Mtshabezi Wenlock area in Gwanda north to make way for White farmers and to build Mtshabezi Mission. My grandfather Tshandiwana relocated his family to Matabo, in the Mberengwa area, where there was open grazing land for his livestock. Most of his family, Mabhada and Makwanya families, stayed in the crowded Wenlock area that was reserved for Black people. Years later, my father's family was again forced to relinquish their land in Matabo area in Mberengwa and were moved to a reservation in Gwanda South. They settled at the first reservation known as Sengezane (Number One). His older brother Siyelani remained in the Matabo area in Mberengwa while the rest of the siblings relocated to Sengezane (Number One).

When schooling was expanded to include Blacks through the Department of African Education, my father had become interested and had asked his father to put him through school. My grandfather had grudgingly agreed as he could not financially support my father. He did not believe in educating children, nor did he trust the government that had forcibly removed his family from their home area. However, my father enrolled at Gloag Ranch Mission in the Bubi area, where he learned carpentry and animal husbandry. He had to support himself by polishing other children's shoes and doing chores in exchange for food and boarding. Due to lack of financial support, he could not continue with his education. He had managed to complete his Standard Four which was six years of formal schooling. The most educated Black people at the time ended in Standard Six. Some Black children would leave school as soon as they were able to read and write, and that was considered educated enough for Black children and qualified them to work for White men.

It was due to his aspiration and interest in education, law, and order that, at the age of twenty-two years, my father had qualified as a police officer under the British South Africa Police (BSAP). He was deployed at the Luveve Police Camp in Bulawayo and quickly rose to second in charge. Due to his Ndebele ethnic background, the White-controlled police staff would not promote him. People from the Ndebele ethnic group at the time were considered confrontational by the White government and were not to be trusted. My hero was later transferred to Ross Camp. Within a few years, he had risen within the police ranks from a constable, a sergeant, senior sergeant, to a sergeant major. Black police officers could not rise beyond sub-inspectors while their White counterparts rose to become chief inspectors and commissioned ranks.

The rise of African nationalism in the early 1960s saw the creation of the National Democratic Party by the nationalists, its banning by the White minority government, and the formation of two national parties, the Zimbabwe African People's Union (ZAPU), under the leadership of Joshua Nkomo (SAHA, 2012) and the Zimbabwe African National Union (ZANU). The Zimbabwe People's Revolutionary Army (ZIPRA) was formed as a military wing of ZAPU, while Zimbabwe African National Liberation Army (ZANLA) was formed under the ZANU party.

The early 1970s had ushered in a new era in the political arena in Zimbabwe. The War of Liberation, also known as the Rhodesian Bush War, intensified between nationalists and the White minority government. Since nationalists were considered as criminals or terrorists by the then government, the British South Africa Police (BSAP) had to adopt a different role to counter "terrorism." Riot standby units were maintained.

As a police officer under the BSAP and a supporter of African nationalism, my father had found himself in a predicament. He would be deployed as a riot standby unit to quash Black rioters or insurgency. Sometimes he would not come home for days. He would be assigned to guard political prisoners, whose values, and beliefs he shared.

One time he was assigned to guard a well-known political prisoner, a union leader and political activist, who also happened to be my father's relative. He brought him home to Ross Camp. Such assignments put him in a predicament. Black police officers resigned or retired in droves during that period.

My hero would be posted for day or night patrol to maintain law and order in various neighborhoods, such as Mokokoba and Mzilikazi, where Black people lived. Makokoba was the oldest suburb. Black people lived on the western side of Ross Camp, while their White counterparts lived on the eastern side of Ross Camp. Crowded housing, air pollution, and unfavorable living conditions marked a difficult life for Black people, while White people lived in large houses. Black police officers often found themselves without patrol cars and would have to walk the streets for patrol or use bicycles. My hero would find himself in this predicament most of the time. Such deployment caused a lot of strain and stress for his family. As a family of an active-duty personnel, we were always on edge, not knowing whether my hero would see another day or not. These were dangerous times and dangerous places, especially for police officers.

Makokoba, where my father was sometimes deployed,

was the poorest township for Black people at the time. The suburb, commonly known as *Elokitshini* (at the location), was built in the early 1900s to house an urban influx of migrant workers. Black people contended with appalling living conditions in this suburb. The construction designs showed lack of humanity by the contractors at the time. The houses were small and so closely attached that one could easily overhear neighbors' conversations. Although originally meant to house only men who worked for White men, the one to three-roomed houses were semi-detached blocks that housed many families. Toilets were built outside and posed challenges at night since the suburb was also dimly lit. Toilets were used at night at one's own risk. Most people preferred relieving themselves in buckets and waking up early enough to dump the urine in the toilet. Others preferred to relieve themselves by the walls if using a bucket at night was an inconvenience. As a result, a pungent smell often rose and lingered in the air for hours.

One of the biggest beer gardens, MaKhumalo Bar, known as the Big Bhawa (big beer garden), was built in Makokoba. This bar attracted many people from all walks of life. It is here where ideas on African nationalism were also birthed. Political activists used the Big Bhawa for their meetings. It was here also that my hero would be on patrol to maintain law and order. It was here, too, that he would also socialize with his peers when he was off duty.

Makokoba was a hive of activity and an epitome of crime, ranging from petty theft to murder. There were people like Smokey, a well-known criminal who lived in Makokoba and had eluded the hand of the law. He had recruited his gang so he could go underground while they terrorized the neighborhood on his behalf. Rumor was circulating that he had escaped to Johannesburg, South Africa. That is what most people were hoping for as they were tired of living in fear. These gangsters would pounce on unsuspecting individuals and snatch their handbags in a flash. They would search all body parts for money and valuables. Slitting someone's throat was no big deal when they felt some resistance or threat. People who resisted or challenged these criminals either succeeded or faced death. Poverty, lack of educational opportunities, housing conditions, and many other issues contributed to such lifestyles among Black people.

The busyness of Makokoba, the poverty, and the crime were indicative of the inequalities brought about by the White minority rule. The culture shock of tribal Africans being thrust into a compound life of oppressive poverty may have had a bearing on their behavior. As different African cultures mingled, it is possible that cultures that devalued others were adopted. It is also possible that such behavior was emanating from the dehumanizing effects of political oppression.

Regardless of the challenges of living in this suburb at the time, there were many success stories. As the oldest suburb, it was home to many legends that changed the course of history, culturally and politically. Legendary artists like Dorothy Masuka graced this place with their music. Nationalists and revolutionaries such as Masotsha Ndlovu and Jason Ziyaphapha Moyo lived in Makokoba. It was here in Makokoba that nationalism was born, which led to Zimbabwe's independence in 1980. Secret meetings were held to concoct plans to deal with the apartheid regime of the then, White-controlled minority government.

As one of the best police officers in his rank, my dad found himself being deployed to such and other suburbs. One day while playing with my friends Francesca, Sylvia, and Addlight, I saw my dad being dropped off home by his colleague. I had not seen him for a week and had been told he was on duty, and he could not come home until the assignment was over. As his little princess, I ran as fast as I could to welcome my hero home and be lifted in his arms. He picked me up and set me down in the living room. He was not wearing his uniform, and his speech was unusual, a bit slurred. I wondered in my six-year-old brain and hoped to get an answer. After taking his shower and changing his clothing, he set down to rest and enjoy supper with his family. I approached him so I could sit on his lap and tell him stories as usual. He was always a jovial person, but that day something seemed to have happened at work that was bothering him. He was not his usual self.

As we set down to enjoy our supper, I noticed that he had bruises on his right arm, and his upper lip was cut. He ate his supper with difficulty but continued to devour it. After supper, my hero opened his mouth, and out came his front teeth. I screamed, jumped, and threw myself in my mother's arms in fear and sadness. Dad had lost four of his upper teeth. My heart sunk, and I sobbed heavily. I had never seen anything like that in my life! In place of his four upper teeth lay this huge piece of dentures. His beautiful gap that most of his children had inherited had been replaced by this one big giant piece of four teeth. It was disheartening. My heart cried out for my hero, my dad, the police captain.

He had been posted for a patrol in Makokoba neighborhood, where his foot pursuit of a robber the previous week had nearly cost him his life. He had just been released from the hospital, and no one had told me! He had received a call about a robbery at Makokoba, where he was on patrol that week. He and his partner had responded to the call of duty. This robber had ignored the call of "Freeze" but had run for his dear life. My dad and his partner had abandoned the police car and pursued the robber on foot. The robber seemed to know his way around, but the two cops outwitted him. They seemed to know where he was headed, and they surrounded him. The robber finally slowed down as he could see that he was being chased by the best athletes in the world.

With gun in hand, my hero had commanded the robber to "freeze" and put his hands up in surrender. The robber did. My hero's partner approached carefully to arrest the robber. Just then, the robber pulled out a chain from nowhere and used it to hit my dad's partner on the head, and he fell to the ground. The robber started running in the opposite direction. My dad pulled his trigger and immediately shot up in the air while pursuing the robber. The robber again ignored the sound of the gunshot and my dad's command but continued running. With his partner laying on the ground, my dad's adrenaline was pumping, and knew he had to get this sucker out of the streets. He pounced on him, pinned him down, but the robber jerked his head forcefully and knocked off my dad's four front teeth. Bleeding all over his uniform, my dad kept his cool while pinning down and arresting this robber. Help finally came, and my dad and his partner survived this incident.

"Ubuzaphetha ngani wena, Smokey?" (How did you think this was going to end, Smokey?) My hero had asked this notorious robber, Smokey, who had eluded the hand of the law for months. Dad was agonizing, spitting blood, and could not even pronounce his "s" due to the missing teeth.

My dad's unit had followed Smokey's tracks carefully. Smokey had been on the police radar for months, and that is why he had decided to lie low. Meanwhile, my dad's unit had spread rumors about Smokey having left for South Africa to make him think that he had fooled the hand of the law. Smokey had believed the rumor and had thought he had eluded arrest. He began to relax and go back to his old ways. Little did he know that he had been outsmarted. The hand of the law had pounced on him as soon as he had emerged from his hiding.

Mr. Policeman narrated this story and would be as animated as ever as he was laughing out loud, chuckling, and demonstrating using his hands. Rolling out with laughter, with tears running down our cheeks, defined my family.

If this laughing gene was triggered while one harbored a full bladder, too bad! Humor and good storytelling were also packaged with this gene. My older siblings and uncle Amon, who was a police cadet at the time, were laughing hysterically. They were clapping and interjecting by praising him using his nicknames. That day, I refused to let this laughing gene take control of my life. There was nothing funny as far as I was concerned. My hero had lost his teeth, and that was traumatic. Although injured, my hero was so proud of himself. He had been taken to the hospital and had spent a week there. His dentures had been expedited, and he was released from the hospital to recuperate at home for a month.

"That wicked witch, Smokey! The devil was charged with culpable homicide and assault with intent to cause grievous bodily harm."

My hero had concluded as he nodded his head. I remembered these charges for a very long time. To me, they were a bunch of tongue twisters. Big words. This incident and many near-death experiences exerted stress and strain on my family. Ours was a waiting game before we could hear worse news than losing upper teeth. The loss of his teeth had led to the loss of his signature *itsako* (diastema), and to me, that had been traumatic. In all this, my mother was looking at dad with awe and obviously wondering what could have happened to her and dad's brood of children had he lost his life. Like many lives of families of active-duty personnel, each day was counted as a blessing.

Caught between African nationalism, his desire to maintain law and order, or serving the interests of White minority rule, my hero found himself in conflict with himself and the world around him. Black police officers were viewed as sellouts by other Black people and always ran the risk of lynch mobs. My family had every reason to be concerned. His coming home in one piece was always counted as a blessing.

We were sitting at the table after supper one day a year after the teeth incident when dad said he had an announcement. We did not think much about it since we were used to sitting down as a family and hearing stories from Mr. Policeman.

"Yeah, I will be retiring at the end of the year. Since we do not own a house in the city, that means that mom and Li will go to our rural home first, and the rest of the family will follow at the end of the year."

"What?" I wondered if I had heard right. Everyone stared at me, and I stared at my hero, who was clearly out of his mind, as far as I was concerned. He drank occasionally, but I was sure he was sober.

"Yes, Li. I cannot continue with this job. The current situation is getting too dangerous. It is hitting too close to home. Mom cannot go to our village alone without you. You know that. She will have to transfer from her current job, and teach at Sengezane Primary School, our local rural school at home. The rest of the family will follow in December." Mr. Policeman concluded.

Yes, back to the announcement. My dad meant that my mother and I were to leave the city and go to our rural home, Sengezane. It seemed to me that the case had already been discussed and decided. Mom and I were to go to our rural home and prepare it while the rest of the family stayed in the city until the end of the year. I could not understand why my mom and I had to have that sentence. I was only seven years old at the time, and I had no control over where I lived and with who. I had been assigned to my parents, or my parents were assigned to me, whichever came first and made sense.

I had just finished my second term of my first grade when my father's retirement was announced, and my sentence was pronounced. I did not like the idea of leaving the city life and my best friends.

If I had been raised in another culture, I would have stood up and looked my dad straight in the eye, slumped my shoulders, stomped my right foot, turned, and went straight into my bedroom. I would have slammed the door, locked myself in, and cried, "Go away!" if anyone tried to persuade me to come out.

This was a blow! My rural home was nothing like the city! I was devastated. My world came crumbling down.

Chapter 5

The Village

The vast barren land and the September sun welcomed my mother and me to our new abode at our village in Sengezane. This is the home where my father's family had been resettled after being removed by the White minority government from Matabo in Mberengwa. Situated about sixty kilometers (thirty-seven miles) south of Gwanda town, this dusty place was home to my extended family on my father's side. My mother and I had come to prepare the home so the rest of the family could join us as villagers at the end of the year. The sun released its fury on us and drenched us in sweat, reminding us of the dry season that engulfed this place. As a dark-skinned girl, I wondered about my "Black is Beautiful" complexion at the end of this unforgiving heat spell. The Bulawayo sun had left me still a "Black Beauty," as I was called. This Sengezane sun, however, was intent on roasting me and turning me into charcoal. Of that I was certain. I wondered what my choices were in this barren land.

Natural landmarks identified this vast barren land. A few scattered hills protruded from the horizon, marking borders for each village, Bhalula, Gumbire, and Bhandane. Tall drought-resistant trees, *umkhomo* (baobab), *amadolofiya* (acacia), *umganu* (Marula), and *umthophi* (Boscia albitrunca) perched majestically atop the brown hills. Mopane trees, *umkhaya* (monkey thorn), and *umtswili* (leadwood) confidently claimed possession of this semi-arid landscape. Thorny shrubs, *isinanga* (acacia pallens), and *umphafa* (buffalo thorn) stood protectively and threatened vengeance on any foes that dared reach out. *Amadolofiya* (prickly pears) thrived in this dry land. Dry thorny shrubs, sporadic tufts of trees, dry acacia, and baobab trees would be seen scattered as far as the eye could see. We did not have electricity in the rural area. Our source of fuel was fire. These dry trees also provided firewood for cooking and to keep us warm.

One of the most notable landmarks was the Thuli River (Formerly Tuli). This great river ran from Gwanda North (Matobo District) to Gwanda South, meandering through her sinuous curves, making loops and turns as she passed through my village. She gracefully separated my paternal village of Sengezane with Ntalale, my maternal grandmother's home. The unforgiving scorching sun had dried her riverbed, the very source of life for the villagers.

Maphakela, a big black boulder, stood firmly grounded right in the middle of the great river Thuli, unperturbed by the sun and the elements that beat down on his bald head. The sight of the great river Thuli and her mate, boulder Maphakela, at this time of the year, brought despair and misery as the vast sand could be seen shimmering under the blazing sun. The only visible water source could be located around Maphakela. Undeterred by the elements, Maphakela would stand exposed but still extend his arms to invite villagers, birds, and animals to share this precious commodity. With the rains, we would use Maphekela as our diving board. But now, glaring at this meandering wonder and her longtime mate, I felt hopelessness engulfing me. I wondered how long the dry spell would last.

The great Thuli River with her mate, boulder Maphakela.

The brown soil, devoid of grass, would spit balls of whirlwind that would erupt into the sky. These balls would cloud the sky with dust and send shivers down my spine. This sight was both spectacular and intimidating to the onlooker. The balls of whirlwind would change direction unbeknown to the onlooker in the wink of an eye and cause havoc to whoever or whatever it decided to twirl on. Many times, people would be left uncovered if they were wearing loose-fitting clothing. It could also lift people and dump them on the ground like a bag of potatoes. At times it would be so strong as to rip off the rooftops and leave people scurrying for cover. Both spectacular and daunting, this phenomenon would resemble a tornado. It was when the damage was of this magnitude that people would begin to speculate about the origin of the whirlwind. Narratives of one villager or the other having power over whirlwinds and using them for witchcraft were conjectured and circulated. It was for that reason that I was taught to point at the whirlwind and rebuke it, letting it know that it needed to show some respect. I would rebuke it and say,

> *"Kithi kulomkhwenyana,"* (We have a son-in-law at home,)

> *"Kithi kulomkhwenyana!"* (We have a son-in-law at home!)

This rebuke was meant to alert the whirlwind that it needs to back off and show some respect because there is a son-in-law at home. At the rebuke, it was hoped that the whirlwind would change direction. I am not sure who came up with such an idea. At least for once, it was not my big brother.

With the rains, Sengezane came alive and displayed a different personality. The rainy season ushered a promise of a bumper harvest. A lush of green beautified the flat landscape. *Ulude* (spider plant), *imbuya* (Amaranthus hybridus), and *idelele* (okra) sprung forth from cattle, sheep, and goat kraals and offered their leafy greens to villagers. Lilies and daffodils announced their presence with their bright color scheme. *Izagenama* (Urginea sanguinea bulb) would issue warnings with their purplish leaves for anyone who dared confuse them with *izadenda*, the edible bulbs.

The few available wild African berries, *izibunduma*, *umpumpulwana*, and *umbhunzu* (Grewia flavescent), would burst forth and extend an invitation to animals, bugs, birds, and humans alike. We would fill up buckets of these wild berries to the brim and feast, knowing fully well what this landscape's personality would look like in the coming months.

Mopane trees stood tall, proclaiming their role as the matriarch of this barren land, and rightfully so. The fierce whirlwind would have carried the mopane seeds as far as possible to ensure the existence of their next generation. While the drought brought sadness to this species, they would be observed springing everywhere once the rainy season started. Mopanes provided fuel as firewood. Their sturdy and trusted wood was widely used as building material for houses, huts, fences, and sculptures. Their dried barks were used to produce dye for various artifacts. Their fresh bark was used to make ropes of different kinds and sizes. They provided some type of honey called *ingongomtshane*, which lodged right inside the trunk.

Most importantly, mopane trees were home to one of the most popular Zimbabwean delicacies, *amacimbi* (edible caterpillars/mopane worms/emperor moth). Around November, Mopane trees would be loaded with caterpillar eggs which would develop into beautiful black and white caterpillars by December/January. Once fully developed, they would be seen crawling everywhere, devouring the mopane leaves, signaling their readiness for harvest. These worms could be as thick as a thumb or cigar and the length of the middle finger. Once they are harvested, the entrails are squeezed out to rid them of the bitterness of the mopane leaves. The caterpillars are then roasted in fire to get rid of the prickly thorns and to help preserve them. Yes, Mopane trees rightfully claimed their role as the matriarch of this land. Oh, hail to the Mopane tree!

Amacimbi (caterpillars/mopane worms) made themselves into our menu. My aunt NaMeji taught me how to devour the creepy crawlies. Her home was surrounded by Mopane trees, so these delicacies would eventually make their way to the ground for their final stage of life. My cousin Tshengi and aunt NaMeji would pick them from the ground and harvest them, and roast them. At first, when eating these delicacies, I would remove the head and tail, later I would remove just the head and finally learned to devour the whole caterpillar. This experience is like eating shrimp, squid, mussels, snails, frog legs, lobster, and/ or other slimy foods for the first time in your life. It can be intimidating and make you wonder why anyone in his or her right mind would eat that.

I am reminded of the children of Israel in the Bible who woke up one day to see what looked like coriander seeds on the ground, and they wondered what that was. They called it "mana," to indicate surprise at the thing. I am sure that is what villagers who first identified *amacimbi* thought. This is mana to a dry, thirsty land.

Birds of many species also emerged to attract the beholder. Birds such as *uJijiyane* (weaver), *uMguwe* (secretary bird), and *uKoro* (Yellow-billed Hornbill) perched on trees while *uDwayi* (secretary bird), *uGure* (plover), and *iwundundu/insingizi* (the ground hornbill) took stock of their surroundings. Famous for their vocals, locals had rightfully named these birds based on the musical rendition of their cry.

UJijiyane (weaver) would lead the choir with her high-pitched soprano. She would tweet and tweet while jerking her body back and forth for effect. Her deafening tweet of "Chirp! Chirp! Chirp!" would pierce through the sky and the dry landscape.

UKoro (Yellow-billed Hornbill) would be heard singing in her baritone voice of "Crow! Crow!"

Umguwe (secretary bird), also known as the "go away bird," would challenge with the alto of "Go away! Go away!"

The *iwundundu/insingizi* (ground hornbill), being the larger of the mentioned birds, would steal the show with the deepest voice of them all. Crowned with the staccato beat of "Wu-ndu, wu-ndu, wu-ndu-ndu!" the *iwundundu/insingizi* would belch it out and produce the most powerfully arranged low notes that would resonate like an African talking drum. This rendition would draw attention to his surroundings and this landscape.

With each bird competing for a spot on the Zimbabwean bird talent show, the musical performance would resuscitate this barren land into a sonata of beauty and awe.

Creepy crawlies such as *umahaqaza* (itchy worm) and *umhogoyi* (green worm) would creep to their destination, aware of the changing personality of this land. Deafening sounds of *inyeza* (cicada) would be heard early in the morning, signaling a bright day, a day of hope. Different species of black ants – *inswintila* (small black ants) and *impolompolo* (large black ants) would emerge armed with venom that would be injected to anyone considered a threat.

The rainy season would also resuscitate the Great River Thuli. The once dry river now flooded its banks and would burble as it traveled south from my village into the Great Shashe River. I would hear it babbling and rumbling while transporting logs and sticks. Different kinds of fishes- catfish, mackerel, and sardines would celebrate this miracle with backflips and breaststrokes. I would marvel at the sight of this great wonder as it smothered like a great mamba snake, threatening those that dared cross over from

Ntalale, my maternal grandmother's homestead, to Sengezane and vice versa. Those that dared defy the looming threat and logic faced the undercurrent wrath of the river. The river would unleash its fury on the unsuspecting, the brave, and the unwise. At this time of the year, Maphekela, the big black boulder, would stand firmly, submerged in the water with only his bald head protruding. This would signify the dangers that loomed beneath the brown waters and announce the end of the deadly dry season.

To cross Thuli River at this point was like committing a death wish. The story of Maphakela, the boulder's name's sake, served as a reminder of this ferocious river's record. Caught right in the middle of the flooded and furious Thuli River, the man named Maphakela once perched right on top of this boulder's bald head and waited for the water to recede. The boulder earned the name Maphakela for saving the man Maphakela from drowning. Flooding unexpectedly, the river would sneak up on the unsuspecting and napping villagers and sweep them with her powerful force.

The great Thuli River.

Scattered homes with round thatched huts, and a few bricked houses, marked each homestead. Many of my extended family lived here. Aunt NaMeji and Aunt NaPhetsheya lived to our north, while Uncle SaElliot and Uncle SaKhali lived northeast of our homestead. My cousins Anna and NaMtswakayi lived south and north of our homestead, respectively. To the east was our neighbor SaKhelina (aka Refa), while his brothers SaThoko (aka Mkhumbi) and his brother Luka lived adjacent to each other southwest of our home. The nearest homestead was about half a mile away.

Villagers did not have to buy a house here; they freely owned the land which was distributed to them by their chief or chieftains. Each family possessed kraals located a few yards near their homesteads to house the livestock such as sheep, goats, donkeys, pigs, and/or cattle. Chickens, dogs, and cats stayed within the homestead to keep the family company and, in the case of chickens, provide the much-needed source of protein. Each family also possessed a field or farm across the main road on the east side of the village. Sandwiched between these homes, our family shared the common bowl that had kept this village alive in this semi-arid landscape. This was my new home now, a semi-arid place with multiple personalities.

The location of our home to the nearest amenities was a challenge. The nearest clinic was about three kilometers away (about two miles). Manama Hospital was about thirty kilometers south of our homestead (about nineteen miles), while Gwanda Hospital was sixty kilometers north of our homestead. The grocery store was about three kilometers south of our homestead (two miles), while the primary school was about three kilometers north of our homestead. In my seven-year-old eyes, these distances were unreachable. The main road was a mile away. Everything seemed to be about a mile or so away. I always had to walk for miles to cover those distances. Bicycles were available for those able to afford and ride them.

There were no toilets in my village. We used the nearest stream or bush to relieve ourselves. I would hide in a valley or gorge, or whatever tree or grass was available for privacy and relieve myself. Here I was also afraid of being eaten by a wild animal such as a jackal, hyena, or beaten by snakes and scorpions. I had to use a stick to wipe my bottom after passing the stool. I had to make sure I was aware of my surroundings in case I mistook a green or brown snake for a stick or accidentally used a stick infested with ants or termites. We would have newspapers sometimes, but they were not readily available. Toilet paper was out of the question, out of our reach.

Our Sengezane Primary School was about two miles north of our homestead. Once registered, I started my third and final term in first grade. I had left Ross Camp without saying goodbye to my friends. My mother had asked for me in class, and I had picked up my book bag and left. No goodbyes. I had gone to one class to bid farewell to my mother's friend and relative, who was a teacher. I was the only one in my family at Ross Camp Primary School at the time.

I joined my class in the village at Sengezane a week after schools had started for the third and final term of the year. The school was far, about two kilometers away from home. We went to school as a group. We would pass through other homes and collect other children so we could walk or run together. Sometimes Tsatsi would accompany me to school and leave me close by, where I would join other children for the rest of the walk/run. After school, we would meet up and walk as a group. The distance was too long for me. I hated it.

My new school went up to seventh grade but had only six classrooms. My first-grade class had to be split in half so one teacher could teach one full class and a half class of first graders. My class spent most of the time outside since we shared the classroom with second graders. We would go to the classroom for a test and go back outside.

I was very lucky and blessed to have Mrs. Siyengo Siwawa as my final-term first-grade teacher. We called her Mrs. Siwawa, but she was also known as Mrs. Fanathi. Either name worked. Mrs. Siwawa was a very good teacher. She also happened to be my aunt. Having Mrs. Siwawa as my teacher was a breath of fresh air. I loved her just as I loved Mrs. Nkandla. She built on the foundation that I had already had, challenged me, and encouraged my creativity. That very term or semester, I earned a spot on the Christmas story from our first-grade text as the main character. I was Mary, the mother of Jesus, and my doll Lilibel acted as Baby Jesus! Imagine the performance! We prepared the performance and presented the skit at the end of the school year celebration party. I still remember the words.

"Uyalala ngokuthula, umntwana wami. (My child is sleeping in peace).

Phupha amaphupho amahle." (Sweat dreams, my child).

My individual performance included a poem that allowed me to showcase my personality. With a voice loud enough for everyone to hear, I belted it out and showed with my hands how I would grow.

Aluba ngangililuba (If I was a flower)

Ngangizakhula (I would grow)

Ngikhule (and grow)

Ngithi, "UThixo uyangithanda!" (and say, "God loves me!")

"UThixo uyangithanda-a-a!" ("God loves me!")

There was no Ndaba to shove down the hill. And the words of the rhyme did not allow any pushing down the hill. I had to contend with that. Short as I was at the time, I would extend my hands for the growing part and stand on my tippy toes. I would tilt my head to the side (as I always do) and look up to the heavens to demonstrate the "God loves me" part. My hero was there, proudly watching his dearest daughter doing what she loved doing- performing.

There wasn't much entertainment at Sengezane, with the absence of the brood. Since my siblings were still in the city and I did not have them to hang around with, I spent most of my time studying. Mrs. Siwawa had taught me to understand the pattern in our isiNdebele orthography. I studied the sound system and how to spell even the most difficult clusters like *"tsh," "ntsh,"* and *"ntshw,"* and clicks like *"xh," "gq," "nc,"* and/or *"gcw."* By the end of the year, I had mastered most of them. I came top of my class. I was where I was supposed to be.

Sengezane Primary School.

Chapter 6

The Villagers

After her transfer from Bulawayo to our rural home, Sengezane, my mother could not find a teaching position at the local school for that final term. She then took a teaching position at another village, Pelele, as a relief for one of the teachers who had gone on maternity leave while waiting for her position to open at the beginning of the year. Pelele was about sixteen kilometers (ten miles) away from home. I saw her on weekends. Mother would ride her bike back and forth since it was the most readily available mode of transport at the time. I was left under the care of my cousin Tsatsi and Uncle James.

My cousin Tsatsi (her name means sun) came to live with us and took care of me before the brood joined us. Her father, SaKhembo, was my father's older brother. Since our fathers were siblings, culturally, she was considered as my sister, more so than my cousin. She was six years older than me. She would make my dolls' clothing. She would take me to the grocery store to buy shoes. Her love and tender heartedness made my life bearable as she took care of me during my family's absence.

Tsatsi and her friends Chithekile and Eva would arrange to go to the great river Thuli to fetch some water during the late afternoon. I would be invited to join them even if I would not carry water on my head like they did. We would get to the great river Thuli and approach Maphekela, the only available water source. I would observe Tsatsi identifying a dry place next to the big boulder Maphakela and would start scooping the sand to make a big round well. The water would fill the well. To filter it, Tsatsi would scoop until clear water filled up. I would admire Tsatsi and the village girls, Chithekile and Eva, carrying buckets of water on their heads.

By the time I was in second grade, I was able to read novels fluently in my isiNdebele language. To keep myself busy, I conducted private lessons and taught my neighbors and agemates, Sifiso and Bancane, how to read. I would act as a teacher and write on the ground with a stick or on a rock using charcoal. I would have charged exorbitant prices had I known and understood my position at the time.

One weekend, my cousin Tsatsi took me with her to watch a soccer game between the local boys who played for entertainment and competed against another village. The local team was under the sponsorship of Stanley Noble, the local grocery store owner. A fight broke out during the game, and one guy threatened his opponent with a knife. I watched in horror as people struggled to separate them.

The following week, Mrs. Siwawa asked us to write a story during our news and stories time. I wrote the story about the fight and decided to illustrate with a drawing. Mrs. Siwawa liked the story and the illustration so much that she thought it was worth reading to the whole school. I was surprised but elated. My story was read at assembly, and I instantly became a celebrity. The seventh-grade teacher at the time, Mr. Nleya, invited me to pose with his seven graders as they took a picture to celebrate their graduation from primary school. That is the only picture I have as a memory of Sengezane.

Most of my father's siblings and their families lived here at the village. Just like the brood, my father's family also shaped my life one way or the other. I was one of the youngest of all cousins in this area.

As a side note, culturally, adults were addressed as mother of their first-born child or father of their first-born child. The prefix used is "Na" for mother of and "Sa" for father of. For example, since my dad's first-born is Emmanuel, my barber brother, dad was addressed as "SaEmmanuel." My mother was addressed as "NaEmmanuel." This is a cultural norm. Culturally, adults' names remained unknown to most people, including family members in some cases. Adult women, whether married or single, were also called by their maiden's name. The prefix "Ma" is used for females, as discussed previously. Married males could also be addressed using just their last names. This was a cultural way of showing respect to elders.

My eldest aunt NaPhetsheya (Mother of Phetsheya), the first born in my father's family, lived with her family less than a mile from our home. She was the most fascinating woman I have ever known. Stories regarding her are endless. My mother nicknamed her "MaFusha," meaning "a woman who dries and preserves vegetables." My aunt was famous for drying and preserving vegetables in preparation for the winter and dry season ahead. She would cook, dry, and preserve vegetables such as *indumba* (bean leaves), *ibhobola* (pumpkin leaves), *idelele* (okra), *imbuya* (Amaranthus hybridus), and *ulude* (Cleome gynandra).

Since my first-grade class ended earlier than other grades, I would go home earlier. My aunt's home was nearer the school than mine. I had to pass by her place before getting home. Instead of just walking past her home, I would stop by to chat and hopefully get something to eat. I would announce my presence, and she would send me away by saying that I should pass on in my hungry state because she had nothing to share with me. She would say,

"Dlula ngendlala zakho ntombi!" (Pass on, my dear girl, in your hunger. I have nothing to share with you!) she would announce.

The first time I heard her say that to me, I was shocked because she was eating! I had learned to share whatever I had. Eventually, I accepted the situation. She would say the same thing whether she was eating or not. I reported this behavior to my family, who made fun of it. The statement became my family's motto each time someone was eating something pleasant.

Our Sengezane was a place of *i-tho-tho-tho*, some illicit beer made from fermented sorghum seeds and sugar. There are many concoctions that can be added to *i-tho-tho-tho,* to make it spicy and more addictive. Some people add poisonous tree sap like that of *ingotsha* (African Milkbush or Pencil Cactus). According to Dias (2014), its alcohol content can be over eighty percent, compared with traditional brews, which have between one to eight percent. The sorghum is left to ferment for about three to five days. This beer is addictive. It got its name from the sound it makes while dripping from a distillation trough, drop by drop. The sound "Tho! Tho! Tho!" is made, hence its name. If poured on a piece of meat, it cooks it immediately. People who drink it normally lose weight and become alcoholics and are likely to die of liver cancer.

Our neighbor NaKhelina was the queen of *i-tho-tho-tho* brewing. I do not remember a time when this brew was not made at her home. She would give us *umhiqo* (the porridge before fermentation) to drink. This is fermented porridge in the early stage of *i-tho-tho-tho* preparation. I once tried NaKhelina's *i-tho-tho-tho,* and the experience was unpleasant. It burned my tongue and lips, and I could not even swallow that poison. It took me a while to even open my eyes. For a moment, I thought I was blind. I was eight years old at the time. I knew that day that *i-tho-tho-tho* was not for me, maybe later, but not for now. NaKhelina was preparing us to be young *i-tho-tho-tho* drinkers, but I had failed the test.

There was not much to do at the village, so most adults spent their times drinking *i-tho-tho-tho* wherever it was sold. My aunt MaFusha drank *i-tho-tho-tho* most of the times. She would walk all the way to her home with eyes closed while pointing the way and singing or crying, "Hee, hee, hee, hee, hee, hee!" She was a pro at finding her way. We were always amazed at her navigation skills. During *i-tho-tho-tho* drinking at NaKhelina's home, the patrons would also dance to the beat of drums.

My aunt also smoked tobacco, the kind that one would put under the tongue, chew, or sniff. That stuff she shared with my cousin Tshengi, brave sister Thando and me constantly. Yes, the same aunt who would tell me to pass by on an empty stomach shared her tobacco with me. It made us sneeze, and we would ask for more.

As the oldest sibling, my aunt knew my father's family history in detail. She taught me our praise names/totems, and she would be heard saying:

"eMaphosa!

eNkala!

eTshele!

eNoko!

eNsuma!

eGubulamleje!"

Like most Zimbabwean clan names, our clan's name Maphosa is derived from an animal. The praise names are a combination of isiNdebele, isiJawunda, and SeSotho, languages spoken in the region of Gwanda, where my family's ancestors had settled. These praise names or totems are based on characteristics of a porcupine, suggesting that as a clan, our behavior resembles that of a porcupine. Porcupines are large rodents that are covered in sharp spikes or quills. When protecting themselves, they inject those spikes to the enemy and cause grievous bodily harm and psychological torture. Psychological torture comes about because one would have underestimated the rodent. Imagine a lion or a leopard in the Savana, or a dog in the yard, trying to attack a porcupine! The results have never been pleasant. Based on this observation, my ancestors succeeded in instilling courage, self-esteem, confidence, and building unity among future clan members.

Then there was aunt NaMeji who was the second born in my father's family. She was hard of hearing, but we all knew how to communicate with her. I spent most of my time at aunt NaMeji's place. Her son, my cousin Meji (Major), lived and worked in the city and did not come home regularly. He and his wife NaZacharia had four children, three boys and a girl, Sitshengisiwe (Tshengi for short). I played with Tshengi.

My aunt and her daughter-in-law, NaZacharia, both drank *i-tho-tho-tho* and were always quarreling. NaZacharia would drink *i-tho-tho-tho* beer and not look after her children, leaving all the responsibility to my aunt. One day she was so out of her mind due to *i-tho-tho-tho* that she quarreled with her mother-in-law as always and spit in her food. They started fighting, and she took a smoldering log and threatened to burn the grass-thatched hut we were in. Had it not been for my cousin David, who was passing by, we would have perished in that hut. She picked up her youngest child at the time, put him on her back, and left to live with her family in another village. That was it. She never looked back.

Uncle SaEliot was my father's second brother, the fifth born in the family. He earned the nick names John Walker or John White from my big brother. He, too, drank *i-tho-tho-tho* and other alcoholic beverages. He had two sons, Elliot and Nothani. Elliot had intellectual disabilities, and yet he was the sweetest cousin of all. Nothani was a year younger than my sister Nhlanhla and a year older than my sister Thando. Because of his age, he fit in right between my two sisters as if he was our sibling. As a result, we were constantly with him. I adored my cousins as if they were my siblings. I would follow Cousin Elliot everywhere, if given a chance. I liked visiting my uncle's home.

There are many times when our Sengezane experienced severe drought. One time, the drought was so severe that most of the cattle died due to lack of food and water. Uncle SaElliot slaughtered one of his cows before it succumbed to the drought. This was the first and last time I remember a cow having been slaughtered within my family confines. Our neighbor SaThoko slaughtered cows all the time. We had always slaughtered goats and shared them among my aunties and uncle SaElliot's home. At the end of the goat sharing, my family would be left with a small piece to last us no more than a week. So, this time, Uncle SaElliot slaughtered his thin drought-stricken cow. My sister Nhlanhla, known as "one with a small heart," could throw up at the sight of a fly. This time she threw up her intestines! I could not help it too. Maybe I threw up my gall bladder! The taste of that meat! The smell! Oh my! The smell was repugnant and revolting. The rubbery meat could not be chewed. Coming from a line of chefs, they could do nothing to make me eat it. That is how severe the drought could be at Sengezane.

Since we used firewood for cooking and to keep us warm, each day, ash would be dumped in an ash pit or dump pit to make room for a new fire. I would find myself in the ash/trash pit for many reasons. I would get the ash and use it as paint. I would also retrieve some items for use during playtime. My constant visit to the ash/trash pit led to crusty and scabby sores on my head. I could not wash my head without feeling pain.

The sores took the liberty to wreak havoc on my head. To relieve the pain, Uncle SaElliot suggested a haircut, a clean shave. The mention of haircuts caused my body to shiver. Many people had tried to kill me through this process, and now my dearest uncle was suggesting the very procedure that made me cringe! I could not believe it. I shuddered! This time, Uncle SaElliot had to do the deed and join the list of those who had tried to cause brain damage through this procedure.

I had faced an electric shaving machine and a pair of scissors. This time I came face to face with a razor blade! With Uncle SaElliot at the realm of this procedure, I saw the end of my life unfolding right before my eyes. Unfortunately, none of my family members were available for me to bid them farewell at this point. I knew my day had finally arrived. I could imagine blood oozing down my head, my cheeks, and all the way down to my feet. I trembled. If I thought barber brother was *inkume* (yellowish scorpion), now here I was with *igungubudza* (black scorpion)! Uncle SaElliot was a no-nonsense man.

An *umandobo* (curved wooden stool) was brought before me, and I was commanded to sit still on it and make no "silly movements," or else the razor blade was going to cut my head and the sores. I followed the instruction and sat motionlessly for the procedure.

My hair had already been washed. Uncle SaElliot lathered my hair with soap. The procedure started. I held my breath and prayed that I would have one more week of life to at least see my mother, who was coming home the following weekend. With the razor blade in his right hand, Uncle SaElliot tenderly held my perspiring little face with his left hand. Starting systematically from my left front to the back, Uncle SaElliot worked his magic. Through the corner of my eye, I could see my hair falling on my shoulders. Before I knew it, he announced with a big smile and open arms,

"It is over, MaTshele! This will help heal your sores quickly." MaTshele is a female name derived from my totem Tshele.

And it was over. I had not bled to death! I was still alive! My uncle was the best razor blade barber of all time! The best barber ever! He had not even touched those scabs with his razor; he had carefully maneuvered around them. I did not have to flinch! I did not even have to hold my ear. Uncle SaElliot had held my ear tenderly and moved his razor blade carefully behind it. Had barber brother been given the chance of razor blading me, I am sure that would have been the end of my short life. Facing a black scorpion was not bad after all, that is, if you were wearing the right shoes! Seating still and following Uncle SaElliot's instructions saved my life.

His wife NaElliot was nicknamed MaVundeka (The Hoarder). She earned this name from the crown prince, my brother, due to her hoarding habits. She would hoard anything and everything from food to clothing. She would hoard *umfushwa* (dried vegetables), *umhwabha* (dried salted beef), and all sorts of produce. I would go there knowing well there would be something new and old to try. New to me but old since it would have been collected a year or so prior.

She would pound sorghum and make it into *isitshwala (pap/polenta/sadza/ugali)*. The process of pounding this crop into flour was fascinating. Unfortunately, I had one problem. Bearing in mind how the village sun beat on the villagers, it was given that body odors would be emitted. That was one of the reasons I hated sorghum. I could not distinguish between body odor and the smell of sorghum.

My two uncles, Mpande and James, were already taking care of our home while we were in the city. Mpande was a cook and had a job as a chef nearby. He would cook anything, and it would taste good. He came home some weekends after work.

Uncle James was a hunter, fisherman, and fowler. He spent most of his time outdoors in the field, in the bush, or at the Thuli River. He would catch anything from a warthog, impala, buck to fish and birds. I loved my uncle James just as much as I loved all my uncles. My uncle James was one person who did not love to bathe. He did not see the value in bathing, or he simply did not have the time for it. Between the hunting and fishing, and herding cattle, there was never a good time for him to take a bath. Not even at night because he would be tired and trying to figure out his next activity. He would come home exhausted most of the time. Because he was always out in the sun, he had a body odor that bothered me. I was never sure if the odor was him not bathing or it was the animals, the fishes, or the birds that he always caught. Because I could not distinguish his body odor from that of his catch, I found game meat and/or fish repugnant.

As a man of the bush himself, a hunter, fisher, and fowler, my uncle James often found himself hungry. He would feed himself on whatever the land provided to him. One day, while doing his business as usual, he stumbled on a wild berry tree known as *umthophi* (boscia albitrunca). This wild berry tree has soft edible berries that melt in the mouth. The berries have small seeds that can easily be swallowed. Hungry as Uncle James was, he devoured the berries and the seeds. He got home and wondered why he was constipated. He did not think much about it until later when he went to the bush toilet.

No matter how much my uncle tried to relieve himself, nothing could be released through that outlet. He tried for an entire week without success. He found himself with no choice but report the cruelty of those berries to his brother Mpande and my brothers Emmanuel and Shepherd. The boys could not help and thus had to ask the help of our other older uncle, SaKhali. To prepare for the surgical procedure to be conducted by SaKhali, James had to drink milk to soften his stool.

Using an okapi knife, Uncle SaKhali cut two small branches of the mopane tree and curved one into a spatula and another into an arrow. Armed with a Mopane spatula and a small arrow to poke and scoop the solid poop, Uncle SaKhali began the operation. On his knees, with pants down and face on the ground, the patient Uncle James prayed he would live through the surgical procedure. With an insurmountable task before him, Uncle SaKhali moved with precision and worked painstakingly through each poop scoop until he reached the soft poop.

Just as he reached the soft poop, an explosion occurred! Without warning, the poop had erupted and flown all over Uncle SaKhali like a volcano. Everyone fell to the ground for different reasons. Uncle SaKhali fell backwards as he was hit in the face, chest, and hands by the flying poop. His spatula and arrow went flying and fell to the ground somewhere. With the release of the seeds and the acidic waste, James fell limply on his side as he groaned in pain. As his poop was released, his stomach celebrated its independence from the notorious *umthophi* berries. Hearing the indefinable sounds, and seeing SaKhali's condition, Mpande and my brothers could not hold themselves; they fell to the ground with laughter. My father's laughing gene had been triggered, and there was no stopping it.

The thought of *umthophi* berries, SaKhali and James, triggered giggles for a very long time. From that time on, I revered that *umthophi* tree and her berries and did not come near them, no matter how enticing they were, until I was much older. That was my uncle James and his saga.

With the absence of my mother, my hero, and the brood, my village banded together and raised me. With the help of my babysitter, cousin Tsatsi, Uncle James, my beloved teacher Mrs. Siwawa, cousin, and friend Tshengi, my aunties NaPhetsheya, NaMeji, and NaElliot, and Uncle SaElliot, I was ready to face challenges presented to me by my new environment. I was becoming a village girl. As I eagerly waited for the brood and my parents to join me at home, I knew that I could never walk a mile alone.

Chapter 7

The Reckoning

As the brood and my father joined us at Sengezane, it became apparent that the following year was going to be a challenge. Schooling the older children meant sending them to live with relatives in the city. With no house in the city and limited resources to put them in a private school, it meant that the brood would have to stay with relatives in the city so they could complete their high school education at Mzilikazi High School. The three younger children, Nhlanhla, Thando, and I, attended the local primary school. Nhlanhla would have to live with another family as soon as she qualified for her secondary education. We faced the new year with uncertainty. New schools. New homes. New families. It was times like these that I learned the true meaning of love. I had my family, village, and friends to journey with me.

My mother had the honor of being my third-grade teacher at Sengezane Primary School (haha!). That was fun. It was my best term ever! She was my favorite teacher with

Mrs. Siwawa, of course. My mother was a kind, patient, and intelligent teacher. I never forgot one lesson she taught us. She first asked us what a banana was, and I had said it was food. The answer was correct, but she had wanted us to classify it. I was confused because I had never thought that food could be classified. It had never occurred to me that bananas and apples could belong to one group. I just knew them as separate foods that I enjoyed. The shock came when my friend and classmate Nomusa classified it as a fruit. The fact that someone knew the answer and I did not shocked me. I justified Nomusa's knowledge of the answer by the fact that she lived at the clinic with her aunt Nurse Maphosa; she had to know that classification.

My mother, the teacher also, taught me how to classify animals into cats and dogs. I found it silly, though, to classify a lion as a cat. The king of the jungle was not as close to a cat as I was made to believe. For starters, a lion lived in the jungle, and a cat lived at home or somewhere near our old toilet at Ross Camp. A lion was big, and a cat was small and cuddle. I was confused, but I couldn't argue with my teacher, she was the smart one. The classification business made no sense. And most of our traditional foods were not included on the list of foods for classification!

I enjoyed lining up with my classmates to get our work graded by my mother. I would first stand right behind the student whose work my mother would be grading and hear her feedback. I would then quickly erase the wrong answer and write the correct one and then go to line up for my feedback. The surprising thing is that she would see where I would have made an edit, and she would tell me to stop cheating. I would wonder how she figured it out. She would not let me cheat in her class nor let me call her mom!

Mother also taught me to write in cursive. I could not make those loops and hoops, but Mother's patience, guidance, and encouragement made it possible to learn that difficult style. I preferred print writing. I found it easy to make nice circles and lines than loops and hooks. I was glad when it was decided to abandon script, and the schools went back into print writing.

During the school holidays, Mother kept herself occupied with her hands and taught villagers to knit, crochet, bake, cook, and be independent women. She introduced clubs for women where they could compete at the annual cattle sale pens. She would win a prize each time she competed.

To keep himself busy, my hero turned to farming, his second passion. He bought and sold chickens for eggs and broilers for meat. We were taught how to care for the chicks and chickens and how to collect the eggs. There are times when I would be sent home with someone to get someone's order at home. He would send the many cartons of eggs to Gwanda, our nearest city. My hero also bought pigs and piglets, fed them, and sold them. Our goats were the first ones in the village to have earrings for easy identification. He also bred sheep. Since we already had cattle, he bought more to fill the size of his kraal.

With the retirement, fees and tuition requirements, and children living with different families, my hero found himself unable to cope effectively with the stress. The problem solver, the pillar, the responsible and revered man, dulled his pain through alcohol. He joined his brother, uncle SaElliot, his two sisters (NaPhetsheya and NaMeji), and the villagers in drinking the most lethal, locally brewed alcoholic beverage known as *i-tho-tho-tho* for the dripping sound it makes while being distilled. The law enforcer turned into an alcoholic right before our eyes. With his life spiraling out of control, we watched in grief and sadness. He had saved many, but no one could save him. He could not save himself.

He would go to the city to sell his produce and drink all the way back home. He would get off the bus, and it would take him a while to get home from the bus stop, which was less than a mile away. He would be seen staggering, stumbling, and swaying from side to side, trying to make his way home. Jovial as always, he would be singing at the top of his voice, cracking jokes, and making people around him laugh. He had joined the villagers. He had become one of them. His desire to be the bright and shining star had crumbled. Since he was one of the most respected and loved villagers and a larger-than-life character, he would easily get someone to accompany him and make sure he got home safely.

He would be heard singing his own made-up praise names.

"Yimi uJ.J. uphondo olubomvu!" (I am J. J. the red horn!)

"UJonathan!" (Jonathan!)

"UJackaranda!" (Jackaranda!)

By the way, J.J. are his first and second initials standing for Jonathan Jonah. That is how he was affectionately known in the village and in the city. He also gave himself the name "Jackaranda." The rest of the praise names cannot be written here nor uttered due to their vulgarity. He only uttered them when drunk. A hangover the following morning meant he had to hunt for an early brew to relieve himself of a hangover. The cycle continued. His body deteriorated. His family feared.

He also became a chain smoker. He would smoke one cigarette after another nonstop. He would smoke tobacco in its different forms, depending on the availability of the tobacco and the money. He ate less. He drank more. And he smoked more. His body weakened due to the chemicals injected into his once strong body. His skin tone changed from light complexion to brick red. My hero, my father, was in a trap that seemed to be pulling him down with his every move. He was stuck.

My father's drinking habit, having a diabetic child, and challenges of having her children live with other families sent my mother into desperation. My mother could see the direction that her husband was headed. She could see the destruction of the empire they had built together, and she was afraid. Each time my hero was drunk, he and Mother would argue more and more in our presence. He would be downplaying or disputing everything my mother would be saying. He would be insulting her, trying to emerge as a hero. Only my mother could confront him, hence the arguments. He would turn to us and tell us a good story to try to make us laugh as usual. We would still laugh but were scared of the direction he was taking.

Seeing no change, my mother decided to leave him with his brood and go to her family in Ntalale village across the Thuli River. Culturally, since lobola (the bride price) had been paid, she could not take the children with her. The children belonged to my father, according to the culture. But having had enough and wanting to teach him a lesson, she had decided to leave him, anyway. I remember the chaos that ensured as she was packing her clothes. My dad was trying to stop her from leaving, and she was yelling and crying. She could not be stopped. Once she made her mind, it was difficult to change it. She was packing her clothes and ready to live when one of my aunts came and pleaded with her not to leave. It was then that she calmed down and reconsidered.

My father was deep into drinking; he could not stop. To show his desire to change, he found a job as a dip supervisor at the Wenlock/Mtshabezi area in Gwanda North, where his extended family, the Mabhada and Makwanya, and other family members lived. His position was to ensure that each villager's cattle were dipped to avoid the spread of ticks and other pests. We would see him infrequently then. He would drink during his bus ride back home, and by the time he got home, he would be as drunk as a skunk.

It was in 1974, two years after leaving the city, that my mother got a position to teach at Sukwe Primary School, a school about forty kilometers south of our village Sengezane. We had never heard of the place, indicating how remote it was. One evening, dad got the family together for some news.

"Your mom and I have something to tell you," he had started. "I went to visit mom and check out the place where she is teaching. She had been telling me how beautiful it was, and I had to see it for myself. The place is heavenly! The land is virgin land. We have already acquired a homestead and built a round thatched kitchen as a start. We will build more huts and houses as soon as we get settled."

We were all shocked at the news. How we could leave our extended family behind and relocate to some unknown place was shocking. We would have to leave our uncle SaElliot and aunt NaElliot and cousins Elliot and Nothani. We would leave behind aunties NaPhetsheya and NaMeji and cousins David, Charge, and Tshengi. What about uncles Mpande and James? No, that was not going to happen. We had my mother's family, the Mabangas, across the big river Thuli in Ntalale. That was unimaginable.

"This means that we are moving out of this land by the end of the month, that is, in two weeks!" concluded dad. That declaration came in the middle of December. It meant that we were going to celebrate Christmas and New Year and leave at the beginning of 1975.

We all looked shocked, and a quick glance at the matriarch indicated we wanted to hear her side of the story. She met our gaze and cleared her throat.

"Yes, dad and I have agreed that living here is not helping us. This is a dry desert land. The rain is sporadic, and our livestock is not doing well. Where we are going is a rich land. The soil is good for the crop. The people are friendly and generous. They value education, which is important. The school is headed by one of the best headmasters in the region, and the teachers are the most dedicated I have ever known. I know for sure that Thando and Lindi will love the primary school and perform to their best capability. One of the best mission schools, Manama Mission, is not far from the place. You will go there for your secondary education. So, please keep this to yourselves and do not spread it; it is your secret," concluded the matriarch.

"I have already talked to SaBhatha, our neighbor, and asked for his son Patrick and my cousin Musolini to take the livestock. They will have to herd them by foot all the way from here to Sukwe. We will put the chickens in a chicken coop and put them in the scotch cart since they cannot walk all the way," chuckled the patriarch.

That last statement eased the tension, and everyone burst out laughing.

"Patrick knows the back roads, so that should not be a problem. It is about thirty kilometers from here to our destination. That should be a whole day's journey on foot. The boys will leave first thing in the morning and arrive about six in the evening," the patriarch concluded as he twirled his mustache.

My parents had planned the move without letting any one of their children know about the plot. We were going to leave behind aunties, uncles, a grandmother, cousins, and friends and go to an unfamiliar "land of milk and honey." It sounded too good to be true. This sounded like a story I had heard from Sunday school. It was hard to believe. We were going to start afresh after two full years at Sengezane. At this point, it looked like we were nomads, a family of no fixed abode.

And indeed, two weeks later, the brood and the matri-arch boarded a bus to our new destination. As we were at the bus stop, I could not look back. I was afraid of turning into a pillar of salt, like a woman called "Lot's wife" that I had heard of at Sunday school. I did not want to put my mother into a position of having to decide whether to look back or leave me behind as a pillar of salt. The bus came, and we left and never looked back! No goodbyes to my friends and extended family. I had done the same thing at Ross Camp two years earlier. This seemed to be my exit style. No goodbyes, just leave.

Chapter 8

The Move

I woke up to the burbling sound of creeks and rivers and immediately wondered about the events of the previous night. I stretched my cramped legs as I yawned. The fresh, crisp air entered this mud hut through the unfinished rooftop and the two mud hut peepholes, known as windows. The rising sun, adorned in its golden glory, cast its fingers through the mud hut window and ushered in a new beginning. The melodic sound of birds alerted me to my surroundings. As I looked at my mother and snoring sister Thando, I meditated on the events that had led to this sleeping arrangement. The previous night had welcomed us to this remote village in style. I wondered if that had been a good sign or a bad omen.

My family had arrived the previous day from Sengezane, a village we had called home for decades. We had boarded a bus headed to Buvuma, which is about twenty-three kilometers west of Sukwe. We arrived at the Buvuma Business Center by late afternoon. As we got off the bus, we saw Patrick and *"Uvulamabhetshu,"* our don-key-drawn scotch cart, waiting to pick us up. Mother had arranged with one of the storekeepers to keep some of our furniture until we could pick it up at a convenient time. We got into the scotch cart and headed to our destination, our new home in Sukwe. Our exit from Sengezane had been like a great escape, and now we were clinching closer to our secret hideout.

A vast lush landscape greeted us on our way to our new destination. We would come upon a village tucked away in some remote corner, and then suddenly, a vast forest would appear. This pattern repeated itself constantly for what seemed like an eternity. The beautiful cocktail blue summer sky and her hot sun offered a welcoming gesture. After traveling for about twenty-three kilometers (fourteen miles) on a scotch cart, we finally came to what would be our home. We were greeted with two incomplete round mud huts and a yard full of thick grass. The kitchen, near-ing completion, was missing the rooftop. The other one had not yet been roofed. Big brother Emmanuel and the boys immediately tightened the doors. We unpacked what we could for that day. Since it was already close to evening, we made a fire and prepared a single meal for that day. The boys were going to use the other hut while the girls and mom were going to sleep in the kitchen hut.

Just as we were settling down for the night, the sky suddenly darkened into gravel grey. Heavy clouds enveloped the entire horizon and issued a warning threat to those who were unsheltered. The boys abandoned their unfinished "shack" and made a beeline to our kitchen/bedroom/lounge hut. A remarkable showdown between the roaring thunder and blinding bright bolts of lightning loomed in the sky and threatened to torch the mud-built and grass-thatched hut. Fire crackled under the incredible spell of the raging lightning bolts. Displays of amber illuminated the hut, issuing a sight to reckon with. A few thick droplets started petting the roof. Before we knew it, a staccato beat of endless heavy raindrops was pounding the mud wall and pelting the unfinished roof.

With an open invitation to cause misery, the rain hammered and smashed its way into the hut. A big bucket had been placed on the fireplace to harvest the water. Full as the bucket was at this point, the water started to spill over, forming a puddle. The consistent plunking of the raindrops into the muddy fireplace was reminiscence of the damage this storm could bring. I worried, and I wondered. There had been no such storms at Sengezane. I wondered whether to call this a blessing or a curse.

Since the kitchen's rooftop was missing, there was no place to hide. We scurried and tried staying in one place, but the rain just kept pouring into the hut. We had brought our old, corrugated iron sheets for roofing, so big brother took them and placed them on top of the bed to act as a roof. Mother, my sister Orpha, Thando, and I slept on the bed, and the three boys slept below the bed. It worked!

After what seemed to be an eternity, the hammering and pounding came to a sudden stop. The clouds dissipated into the sky. The moon shone as if nothing had happened. I could hear the humming sound of a distant stream and looked forward to seeing this water source. With the moonlight getting through the open rooftop, it was impossible to fall asleep. All huddled together in our little wet mud hut, I wondered about this type of welcome and what lay ahead.

The following morning, we went to Sukwe Business Center to get a few supplies and bring cousin Tsatsi, who had stayed at aunt NaNdaba's place during our absence. The builder and the boys completed the kitchen that day and worked on the other round hut for fear of being found in the same predicament as the previous night.

There were several villages that made up Sukwe-Jenkwa (also known as Lote), Msalili, and Makompo. Our home was in the Jenkwa village, and our nearest neighbor at the time was SaS'manga, who lived less than a kilometer away. Although not far, the dense thicket made it seem as if we were the only humans alive, in the middle of nowhere. All my eyes could see was a dense forest in all directions.

Mr. Cephas Sibanda, the primary headmaster, lived with his family south of our home in the Lote/Jenkwa village. The Sukwe Business Center, the Sukwe Primary School, and the Msalili village were on the eastern side of our home and close to the main road. Between the Sukwe Business Center and the Sukwe Primary School and my home lay a dense forest that stretched for more than three kilometers (about two miles). I did not know whether to be terrified or to enjoy this extraordinary breathtaking scenery.

Two mountains marked our homestead, Lote Mountain on the west and Intabayotshani (meaning a grassy mountain) to the east. Lote was a steep, flat-topped mountain that rose to a height of about 1000 feet. The insidious mist would be seen hovering above its peak. Villagers revered that mountain. Few villagers dared climb it. Legends of people climbing the mountain and never to be seen again or losing their minds afterward were circulated. My brother Shepherd climbed the mountain in defiance and made a shocking discovery. Human bones had been scattered at the top of the mountain! Big brother climbed with him to prove it. Through research, big brother found that a war had been fought, and the Lozwi people had been massacred by the Ndebele people at some point. This piece of history seems to have been kept a secret to the outside world and the younger generation that lived in the area.

Intabayotshani was craggy, with a lot of rough rocks. The myth was that *iginyambila* (a rock python) made its abode in one of the cavities. One could see large rocks precariously balanced, one on top of the other. Wild fruit trees like *uxakuxaku* (slimy-apple/snot-apple), *umkhomo* (baobab), and *umnyi* (bird plume) would entice the passerby, but the ragged terrain at the foot of the mountain would send a discouraging message. I tried to climb to the top of it one day after school with other children, just to prove that I was a brave little girl. We had not yet reached the peak before someone warned us of a rock python. We had scurried down the mountain and never to go back again.

One of our goats once decided to climb *iNtabayotshani*

in search of greener grass and failed to come down. We could see the goat from our home but were unable or afraid to help her. Mother had called one of our villagers, a professed witch doctor, to perform a ritual to bring the goat home. The witch doctor had come home in his full gear and had sprayed the whole home with some concoctions. The goat was never reunited with her family. She was perched on that mountain for a while, and we would feel sorry for her. It was the strangest sight on that mountain for some weeks before she disappeared.

The small hills surrounded the foot of these mountains and formed an impenetrable path to either of the two mountains. Small hills were also scattered around the landscape. On one of the hills, we found some Bushmen paintings. With the signature ochre and red color, and attention to detail, one of the paintings showed two people with spears pointed at a galloping animal. The presence of those paintings alluded to the fact that the land had been native to the Khoisan people some thousands of years before. The Khoisan, also known as the Bushmen or Basagwa, were hunter-gatherers who are said to have arrived from the south of the continent during the Stone Age. They were dispersed by the arrival of the Bantu people, who were agriculturalists. Surviving generations were almost driven to extinction by the colonialists. They currently populate remote areas of Angola, Botswana, Namibia, South Africa, Zambia, and Zimbabwe.

The myth was that there were high chances of meeting a Khoisan in the area. For that reason, we had to be schooled in manners on how to greet a Khoisan when meeting one. It was assumed that they were generally short in stature, and since they knew how to camouflage, they were likely to appear unexpectedly. If they appeared unexpectedly and asked where one would have seen them, we were to say that we had seen them from afar, giving the impression that they were tall. If one responded by saying that one had just seen them, one faced their wrath and would even be killed. The question and response went as follows:

Khoisan: *Ungibonabonale ngaphi?* (How far did you see me?)

Response: *Ngikubonabonale le!* (I saw you from afar!)

As a child at the time, I did not think much about this scenario. I just prayed that I did not have to meet a Khoisan in case I forgot my manners. I did not even think about the Bushman paintings until later in my adult life.

We had several sources of water at Sukwe. The Sukwe

River provided fresh water to the villagers. Although not as big and famous as the great river Thuli that runs in Sengezane, Sukwe River provided our main source of fresh water. We would dig up a temporary well *(umthombo)* and get water from the Sukwe River. The Sukwe Dam, built before independence, provided the much-needed water for irrigation. The irrigation system helped villagers harvest agricultural products throughout the year. There was *isikotsho*, a communal borehole about two miles away from home, where we got our drinking water. We also had *umgodi* (a well). Mother had hired a professional well digger who had dug a well for her. This well was another source of water, although it was never purified. The water could be used for watering. There was also *umswenya*, a spring of water north of our home. The water ran constantly.

The contrast between Sengezane and Sukwe landscapes was vast. Thick foliage demarcated this landscape. A luxurious green of tall leafy trees, shrubs, grass, and flowers of all kinds and species gathered here in this landscape with one common objective: to adorn this paradise. The vegetation shared an ancient heritage of this landscape and told a story that had not been disclosed. A story of life. A story of hope. And a story of rebirth.

Tall indigenous trees, fully clad in their southern African attire, paraded and celebrated their heritage. *Umbola*
(sickle-leaved albizia, like a Jacaranda tree*)*, *iphane* (Mopane), *umbondo* (velvet bushwillow), *umtshwili* (leadwood), *umkhaya* (knob thorn), and *isinga* (sweet thorn)
trees lived harmoniously in this virgin land. *Umkhomo*
(Baobab), *uxakuxaku* (snot apple, nicknamed as the African
chewing gum), *umphafa* (buffalo thorn), *umwawa* (stych-
nos madagascariensis), *umganu* (Marula), *umganunkomo*,
amaqokotshiyane, and *umthunduluka* all showed off their
offspring and strove for the most desirable and sweetest
edible fruit.

Wild indigenous berries of all varieties, such as *umhagawuwe, umtshekisane, umnyi, ubhunzu, umpumpul-
wane*, and *izibunduma* would be seen spreading out their
fruit-laden branches and inviting all to a banquet feast.
Most of my family members had never heard of or seen
umhagawuwe before. With large *ukhomane* (weaved baskets), we would find our way through the thicket to harvest
the sweetest and tastiest berries. This unwavering beauty
and abundance of exquisite wild fruit made this paradise a
heavenly spectacle.

Grass of all kinds and species grew in this area. Lush

and springy grass, tall, prickly, and sharp grass made its abode in this paradise. People in this land would cut grass and use it for thatching, for weaving baskets, and for making brooms. Cattle would feed for the rest of the year with no need for a supplement or being sent to *emlageni* (a place where cattle are kept during drought seasons for feeding).

Exotic flowers of all shapes and sizes bloomed, blossomed, and illuminated this paradise with their ravishing vivid and enchanting colors. *Iqhude* (Flame lily), lilies of all species, daffodils, rosemary, the hibiscus, and the bougainvillea charmed this paradise with colors of white, purple, pink, red, and yellow. Fresh and fancy fragrances oozed out of these delightful flowers and filled the air. The flowers exuded the most delightful and sweet aroma that entranced my spirit into whole-heartedly loving this unique paradise.

The most colorful, attractive, and acrobatic birds lived in this paradise. *Amathendele* (guineafowl) displayed their signature black and white plumage on the runway. *Isiqo-qodo* (woodpecker) with white and gold lines would pound on tree trunks in search of insects or bugs. *Ifefe* (roller), known for her captivating beauty and kindness through the isiNdebele folklore, would be seen parading in this paradise. With her exquisite blue plumage tinted with a green tinge, a purple chest, brown wings, she would confidently perch the treetops and reminiscence about her crowning as the best bird in show.

Umsilabhundu (whydah), with her bumpy tail that earned her the name, would expose her dark brown wings with white patches, a white underpart, and a red bright bill. *Insendlu*, the Greater Honeyguide, would display her acrobatic skills by leaping from tree to tree branch and flapping her wings. This acrobatic dance would be an attempt to draw attention of a human passerby for either honey or a lurking python.

Rightfully named after her musical call, *uSibagobe* would exhibit her magnificent plumage of a white chest and stomach, black back, black mouth, and red eyes. Several species of *amajuba* (doves) would be found here in this paradise. The largest species, *ivukutho*, would display their grayish dark plumage. One dove species wore a black tie. The smallest species, light gray in color, would be distinguishable by their brown neck. These birds presented a plumage display of exquisite beauty.

Not to be outdone, the birds of prey also lived in this paradise. Owls of all kinds and species made their abode in this paradise. An extraordinary countenance characterized this feared and misunderstood nocturnal bird. With a flat face, large eyes, short neck, and a small sharp beak, these birds would be perched on tall trees in search of food. An owl would be heard issuing loud, clear, and resounding notes that would echo through the night. Superstitious beliefs about owls lingered in my mind, and these musical notes would give me the chills. Since my neighborhood was surrounded by tall trees and grass, it was normal to see an owl during the day and hear its hooting during the night. I had to adjust to accepting this nocturnal bird as part of the paradise family.

Together, these birds of this paradise presented an exuberance and exquisite beauty of unparalleled proportion. With their distinctive musical rendition, these birds would chirp, tweet, trumpet, chatter, and shrill. This musical rendition would awaken my senses, and I would be raptured by their spectacular choral symphony. This paradise indeed testified to the presence of the Creator.

**Intabayotshani mountain as it hovered
behind our homestead.**

Despite this heavenly rapture, there was no one my age nearby to share this experience. There was no one close by to play with at my new village for the first few months. By this time, my dolls had been broken to pieces and had not been replaced. To keep myself busy, like I did at Sengezane before the brood joined my mother and me, I read novels that were used as set books for my older siblings. In fourth grade, I was able to read high school novels in my native language, isiNdebele/isiZulu. Since my other siblings were or had already passed through high school, they brought home their set books, and I could read them. Reading a full novel at my age at the time was not usual. The isiNdebele foundation given by my teacher Mrs. Siwawa had made it possible for me to be able to read and understand isiNdebele orthography, complex as it is. One Ndebele classic novel I read by the time I was in fourth grade was *USethi Ebukhweni Bakhe by N.S. Sigogo*. I also read *"Uhambo Lwesihambi,"* the isiZulu translation of the classic *Pilgrim's Progress by John Bunyan*.

In the evenings, when the livestock was brought home for the night, I would play a recorder to the goats. I would climb the goat kraal and play the recorder. Some goats would listen attentively while others would be shaking their heads and ears as if to stop the music from getting into their ears. I enjoyed watching the goats' reaction to my music. I wondered if they were interested, or they simply did not know what else to do. I got to know the goats by their names and gave them names too.

Names of animals were given based on the animals' personalities. We would be given small animals to nurture. If one was lucky, one ended up with a kraal of animals from just one. My goat's name was Ngqeqe (the Clever One), and his mother was NaNgqeqe (Mother of the Clever One). As a kid, Ngqeqe (the Clever One) had this habit of skipping about after suckling, and that distinguished him from the rest of the pack. I guess since I had been called *"uMahlakanipheni"* (the Clever One), my goats had to take after their "mother" and be more clever than other goats. Thando's goat was uSithutha (the not-so-clever one). I wonder what intelligence test my sister had used to determine her goat's IQ. She had made the diagnosis, and the goat seemed to live up to it. Sithutha, the goat, seemed to be always quiet and uninterested in anything, not even in my singing and recorder playing stunts. She was the unmovable.

Our cattle also showed great personalities too. Due to my brother's influence, I also got to know our livestock's personality. One of our cows, Mbembesi, was a jersey cow, and I had not known that in Sengezane. Mbembesi's son Scotch was a bullock. Mswelanhloko, was an unpredictable female cow. With lots to feed on, our livestock quickly multiplied, much to my father's delight. With lots of milk, we were able to make our own *amasi* (cuddled sour milk) or buy some from the villagers as per our desire. My dad owned a flock of sheep. Unfortunately, all disappeared one day without a trace.

Our field was close to our home. Since we had arrived during the rainy season, we were a bit late in planting the crops, but we did it anywhere. We were, however, unable to plow a big field like we had done at Sengezane. With the help of our neighbor SaS'manga, the family was able to plow the field. Since it was virgin land, our neighbor SaS'manga provided labor and plowing resources to prepare the land.

Unable to control her appetite, one of our cows, Mswelanhloko, somehow opened the gate to the field and had a field day devouring the crop. Had it not been for her neck bell that kept ringing, she would have finished all the crop. Nothing seemed to be going well for that year. Since this paradise had plenty of rains, the maize grew, and we had enough to take us through the year and to the following season from the little field. The field was extended the following year.

There was no *i-tho-tho-tho* (illicit beer made from fermented sorghum seeds and sugar) at Sukwe. My hero, a dip supervisor, did not come home as frequently as we would have liked. While he continued to drink, it was not as frequently as in the previous years at Sengezane. He could not drink as much at Sukwe. Families from the Msalili village focused on educating their children and sending them to Manama High School (Manama Mission at the time), and most families attended the Evangelical Lutheran Church. Families from the Msalili area had a different focus and did not encourage *i-tho-tho-tho* drinking. My hero, however, continued as a chain smoker.

During that year, as if responding to a call, Mkhakhisi Nkomo joined us and pitched his home between SaS'manga and ours. After the death of his father, Mkhakhisi had moved his family and siblings from the Manama area and joined us at Jenkwa village. He and his family owned a lot of cattle, so this land provided a good grazing space for their cattle. For me, this was a welcome addition to the village. Mkhakhisi and his wife MaNdlovu were just starting a family and had a little baby girl with whom I could play.

Because of that, I was a constant visitor to their home.

Another move to the village was SaBenon (Amon Ncube), who built a home south of us. SaBenon was a preacher with the Assemblies of God church. He is the man who had given us bags of corn to help us since we had just moved into a new area. We had been shocked and humbled by this gesture. We had learned to give, but to be given was not a daily occurrence in my family, and thus, the gesture by SaBenon was met with gratitude. While this gesture came as a surprise, it was appreciated and never forgotten by my family. He is the preacher we would hear preaching every night through a megaphone or loudspeaker. In the evenings, we would hear a loudspeaker coming from the Msalili area, and we would climb on top of an anthill that was by the other hut to get a better sound quality. We would hear music and some preaching. Living in the middle of nowhere and hearing a human voice besides ours was a welcome experience. We would wonder who the preacher was, but we would join in the singing as we eventually learned some of the songs.

"Oh, Thina sibambene noSathane, yis' gunqu s'gunqu. x2 (Behold, we are fighting against the devil, it's topsy-turvy.)

S'gunqu- S'gunqu s'gunqu. " x2 (It's topsy-turvy.)

We found this song interesting, particularly the use on-omatopoeia of *"s'gunqu, s'gunqu,"* and we would join in whenever the preacher would start his service. So, when Preacher SaBenon became our neighbor, and we could link the corn/maize-giving, megaphone-preaching, and *s'gunqu*-singing to the face, we welcomed him with open arms. He welcomed us too because he was known in this area and was our first neighbor SaSmanga's son-in-law. Mother was quick to come up with a befitting nickname for the preach-er—*"S'gunqu-s'gunqu"* (topsy-turvy). We later learned that his other nickname was *"Pipiya,"* based on the sound of his megaphone. SaBenon immediately became a sen-sation with my family. He and his wife NaBenon were a likable and generous pair. They lived what they preached. My father found him a breath of fresh air, and they would hang out whenever he was around from his dip supervising job. They would talk about both politics and religion.

SaBenon and NaBenon were also a welcome addition for me because they had small children, Benon, Mehlo-kazulu, and Sibahle. Sibahle was the only girl, and I liked her because I could put her on my back and put her to sleep. SaBenon and his wife also occasionally enlisted the help of NaBenon's young sister, Thobekile, who was my age. Instead of staying with her parents at SaS'manga's, Thobekile stayed with her sister close to my homestead. Living about four kilometers from the main road, Thobekile, at the age of ten years, had never seen a bus. She had never been to school. With my mother's influence, she started school the following year.

The following year, the Ngwenya family (SaZodwa and NaZodwa) moved from Ntabazinduna area in Matabeleland north and built their home south of us, about a mile away. NaZodwa was SaBenon's young sister. SaZodwa and NaZodwa had a large family of seven at the time, with Zodwa as the firstborn, followed by Alice (Ally), Thompson, Samkeliso, Albert, Sakhile, and Sazini. This move brought in older girls. Unfortunately, with a larger family, the older girls, Alice and Zodwa, were always busy helping their mother. Thompson and I were of the same age, but he did not attend school at the time. My mother asked for Thompson to stay with us and help in whatever way he could. He became close to my brother, Shepherd. Alice (Ally) was a year older than me, and we instantly became close friends.

Within a year or two, three homesteads had been

pitched within our neighborhood. But still, no matter where I looked, and no matter the season, I was surrounded by a thick forest. Once the three neighbors joined us, I would visit their homes frequently to play.

In all this, my mother was transferred from Sukwe Primary to Nkalange Primary, one of the neighboring schools. I joined her at Nkalange for a year. Here at Nkalange, I met the likes of Dineo, Sikhethiwe and Siyazi. Here I learned to walk like Dineo, chest up, shoulders up, arms behind, and tilt to the side and limp. As the best netball player, she was the beloved of the school. I also learned their SeSotho language variation, which is different from my mother's SeSotho. It was an interesting year, quite different from Sengezane.

The following year, my mother was back at Sukwe Primary School. As her little angel, I tagged along and enrolled at Sukwe Primary for my fifth grade. I enjoyed my new school Sukwe Primary School. The Headmaster, Mr. Cephas Sibanda, was kind and knew how to challenge the students to work harder. Since some of my classmates also lived in the same village as me, transitioning was not a problem. What I found challenging was the caliber of students. I had gone from first grade to fourth grade without any challenges for first position in my class. Here at Suk-we, I faced the ferocious brains of Sukoluhle, Sikhanyiso, Sefelipelo, Phakamisani, Gladson, and Godwin. I knew I had to fight very hard to make it to the top of the class.

My teacher, Mr. Sebata, was a no-nonsense man. He was nicknamed "Mavonyongedzi" (the destroyer), right-fully so due to his constant use of the threat, "I will destroy you!" We feared him as he lived up to his "destroyer" nick-name. He was known for producing good seventh-grade results, which were required for entry into high school. I guess our fear of him gave us no choice but to do our work. I remember one day when he was teaching us how to write an application letter. Since instruction was done in the English language (except for our isiNdebele language), we must have missed what he required us to do or say. He had asked us to tell him how to start the letter, and he had written the first part of a certain physical address on the board. With a meter-long hose pipe in hand, he stood ready to strike at any time. Everyone in class looked blank, and I knew we were going to be destroyed that day. I wondered if he had given us that address at some time, and I had somehow missed it.

I had survived many situations in my life and wondered if I would survive this one. I had survived being stricken by aunt and first-grade teacher Mrs. Siwawa, the black mamba, and my mother, the cobra. Now I was facing Mr. Sebata, the destroyer, the python. I saw my life coming to an end right there and then. As someone who was in the habit of not raising my hand to answer a question, the "destroyer" looked intently at me to complete the address. With hands covering my head in anticipation of being struck by the "destroyer" and a trembling voice, I whispered the answer. The destroyer looked at me and asked me to say the answer loud and clear as he went to write it down on the board. In total shock and relief, I repeated what I had initially said,

P. O. Box 55

Gwanda.

I had completed the address by making it up. I still do not know whether we were supposed to have made up that address or did he think I gave the correct address. We would not have been in that position had we known we were supposed to make up the physical address. I saved the whole class that day!

Our isiNdebele teacher was Mr. Madume Noko. He and the destroyer were best buddies. He was the quiet one and the shorter one. Side by side, the two of them looked like a giraffe and an impala. I was in sixth grade when some seventh graders would come to me with isiNdebele questions. Their teacher, Mr. Madume Noko (who was my isiNdebele teacher too), had told them that I was the best student in isiNdebele. I was shocked because I had not been aware of that honor. This knowledge exerted a lot of pressure on me, as I had to live up to that standard. As we neared the end of the year in sixth grade, I looked forward to a successful seventh grade.

With Mr. Sebata, the destroyer, and Mr. Noko at the helm of my seventh grade, I knew I would perform well and join my sisters at Manama Mission. I knew these teachers would push me to achieve my full potential. I was ready.

Sukwe Primary School.

Chapter 9

The Call

Most people from the Msalili village went to the Evangelical Lutheran Church and sent their children to Manama High School (formerly Manama Mission which was run by the Evangelical Church) for schooling. Education and religion were important to the villagers. There was no *i-tho-tho-tho* brewing and drinking in the Msalili village. Popular families like the Vellah, the Mebe, and Maqethuka graced the area. My Lote village, on the other hand, had a different vibe. There was no formal church. Few people were educated, except for the Sukwe Primary school headmaster Mr. Cephas Sibanda and his wife, Mrs. Sibanda. *I-tho-tho-tho* brewing took place at one or two villages. The main road and the primary school were more than five miles away. Few children went to school. We were tucked away from the world and surrounded by thickets. No one was ever going to find us.

At this point, Mother would encourage us to go to church while she would not set foot at church. She enlisted the services of a self-proclaimed witch doctor to "strengthen" our home. A date was set for the witch doctor to come and perform his ritual. Fully clad in his gear, the witch doctor would be seen talking to himself and spraying the home with his concoctions. Another date was set for a fully-fledged cleansing ceremony, and that day never came because of what followed thereafter.

With SaBenon as our new neighbor, he invited my family for evening prayer. Mother had been putting it off for some time, promising to attend someday. Then one day, Mother decided we should attend the evening service that SaBenon had invited us to attend. SaBenon's family, mine, and Mkhakhisi Nkomo's gathered in Mkhakhisi's family kitchen hut for the service. Some of my siblings were away from home due to schooling and could not attend. My hero was working away from home at the time and could not attend either. The popular song *"Sibambene noSathane, yisigunqu s'gunqu"* was sung, much to my delight. After prayer, SaBenon stood up to preach.

He put on his glasses and looked to his right, left, and center, and opened his big black Bible. He smiled infectiously, stroked his bald head, and shifted from one side to the other. He cleared his throat briefly and then opened his big black Bible. He greeted us by saying,

"Ngiyanibingelela bathandekayo egameni leNkosi ye-thu uJesu." (I greet you beloveds in the name of our Lord Jesus).

His deep voice commanded respect, and for sure, as soon as he had greeted us, we paid attention to what he was going to say.

"Dear beloveds," started Preacher SaBenon. "Tonight, we will read the book of John, Chapter 3 verses 16, 17, and 18."

He cleared his throat for the second time, then with his deep voice, Preacher SaBenon read the three verses slowly and with emphasis.

"Verse 16: For God so loved the world, that He gave his one and only Son, that whoever believes in Him should not perish, but have eternal life.

Verse 17: For God did not send His Son into the world to judge the world, but that the world should be saved through Him.

Verse 18: He who believes in Him is not judged. He who does not believe has been judged already, because he has not believed in the name of the one and only Son of God."

Preacher SaBenon held his opened big black Bible and asked us to close our eyes so he could ask God to bless His word. We complied, and Preacher SaBenon tilted his head up, lifted his hands, and prayed with a moving passion. When he said, "Amen," I knew I was in for a ride. I had never heard such a passionate prayer before. Preacher Sa-Benon prayed as if he was talking to God as one would talk to his or her father. I was taken aback. I was astounded. I was used to praying that sounded like a chant, the kind that the preacher or evangelist leads and the others follow. The singing, the prayer, and the reading of scripture created a desire in me to hear more. I was also feeling anxious at the same time. I had heard the popular John 3 verse 16 scripture but could not remember ever hearing the seventeenth and eighteenth verses. Although I had heard the popular scripture, it had never meant anything to me. I found myself eagerly waiting to hear what Preacher SaBenon had up his sleeves.

"God is a God of love and grace. He is a God of second, third, fourth ...chances. He loves us so much that He gave His only Son, Jesus Christ, to die for our sins. What love is this that a man would lay down His life for the sake of others... I urge you, beloved, to repent of your sins tonight and ask Jesus to be your savior and to come into your heart. It does not matter what you have done, if you confess your sins, He will forgive you, and you will have eternal life. Your soul will be saved from eternal death...," appealed Preacher SaBenon.

"So, Preacher SaBenon is saying that we are all sinners, but Jesus gave Himself upon the cross so that I would be saved from sin and death. Hmmm." I wondered if I was understanding the message correctly.

After the preaching and the closing prayer, Preacher SaBenon made an altar call. He asked us to close our eyes and raise our hands if we wanted to invite Jesus into our hearts. I closed my eyes but wondered whether to raise my hand or not. I had peeped through my fingers to check if Mother had raised her hands. Since Mother had kept her hands to herself, I had followed suit. None of my family members raised their hands that night. Only our neighbor Mkhakhisi, his wife, and his sister had raised their hands in response to the call. We went home that night talking about the service. We were all amazed at the preaching and the music, and the message. We found it interesting and wanted to hear more. We all promised to attend the following week.

The witch doctor visited to check on his "follower" and found that my mother's stance had changed. He wondered what had happened in such a short space of time.

The following week was different. The whole week I had been wondering about the service and what Preacher SaBenon had revealed to us. The song had been stuck in my mind for a while. I knew I should have raised my hand that first night and hoped that the same message would be preached.

A similar message was preached the second weeknight.

"Do not worry about your neighbor, friend, or family. You are doing this for yourself. Today is your day of salvation. We are *all* sinners saved by God's grace. Come as you are and meet the Lord Jesus now!"

Preacher SaBenon appealed as he raised his arms in an open invitation. He emphasized the word "all," and I knew this time that I had to act for myself. The urge to answer the invitation increased, and my heart started to beat even faster. So, when he asked if anyone wanted Jesus Christ in his or her heart, I felt an undeniable urge to raise my hand and receive Jesus in my heart. But, because my life centered around my mother, I had to make sure that my mother had her hand up first. I peeped through my fingers like I had done the previous night and saw her hand shoot up, and then I followed suit. I did without fear. I could not comprehend everything that Preacher SaBenon was saying, but I knew from the depth of my heart that this was my chance. I needed God. I needed God to save me from an empty life. I needed God to forgive me. I needed God to guard me, as my name means. I needed God to guide me. I needed God to help me. I needed God. This was my chance, and I was not going to miss it like I had done the previous week.

"I see the hands that are raised. God sees your heart. He chose this day for you. You are not here by coincidence. You are here by divine appointment, so you can answer the call. Let God take control of your life..." Preacher SaBenon encouraged.

After putting our hands down, he prayed for us. The feeling I had cannot be explained. I took that leap of faith that Preacher SaBenon had talked about and believed that I was a new person. I had been reborn. I had been renewed. I had been restored.

Preacher SaBenon sang a beautiful song that we were able to harmonize.

"Ngizozifihla ngaphansi kwegazi, (I'm gonna stay right under the blood)

Ngizozifihla ngaphansi kwegazi, (I'm gonna stay right under the blood)

Ngizozifihla ngaphansi kwegazi, (I'm gonna stay right under the blood)

Ngek' uSathan' angishukumise." (where the devil can do me no harm)

I was only eleven years old at the time, and here I was answering to a call to serve Jesus without even understanding fully what it meant. I was content. I knew I had made the right decision. This was special because I was doing it with my family. I did not know what lay ahead, but I was content. I went home with an overwhelming peace that I could not explain. An unspeakable joy engulfed my heart.

SaBenon came home the following day to help us understand the decision we had taken and what Christianity was about. And he would explain the Bible in simple, understandable terms. Before long, Mother surrendered all the items she had bought for ancestral worship. She had bought a red, a white, and a black cloth to appease ancestral spirits. A service was conducted, and the materials were burnt. The service was accompanied by the beautiful song, "I'm gonna stay right under the blood, where the devil can do me no harm." The witch doctor lost a clientele that day. He was never to set foot at our homestead.

During the school holiday, a group of Assemblies of God church members, led by Reverend Geoffrey Mkhwanazi and his wife Masombuka, made the trip to visit this remote place of new convents. Several members came to our remote area for a weekend convention, including a young preacher known as Pastor Rodgers and Mrs. Maggie Mhlanga, a gifted singer. Pastor Rodgers, as we called him, was to support Preacher SaBenon. A church had been birthed in one of the most remote areas on earth, at Lote village in Sukwe. This was an indication that God's grace cannot be limited; it cannot be boxed. It finds you where you are.

The preaching, singing, and giving were at a different level. Mrs. Mhlanga taught us many beautiful songs. Reverend Mkhwanazi made an altar call and asked the audience to raise their hands if they wanted to accept Jesus Christ into their hearts. The rest of my family had already responded to the call except my hero. He had been the least interested. He had seemed doubtful that this was the way to go, but a seed had already been planted through his regular conversations with Preacher SaBenon. He saw the excitement of the family and wondered. That day my hero could not resist the urge to answer the call to follow Christ. It was as if the heavens had been waiting for this one person. That day, my father became a new person. The heavens rejoiced.

After the alter call and prayer, Mrs. Mhlanga led one of the most heavenly-inspired isiNdebele/isiZulu hymns.

"Igama leNkosi liyiyo inqaba (The name of the Lord is a shelter from danger)

Ophephela khona uyakusindiswa, (One who trusts in it will be saved)

Ohleli kulona, akana kwesaba, (One who dwells on it does not fear)

Nokuba umhlaba uzanyazanyiswa. (Although the world may be shaken)

Mhla ngiyokumuka, ngishiye lumhlaba, (The day I will leave this earth)

Igama leNkosi, lithikithi lami. (The name of the Lord will be my ticket)

Khona ngizohamba, ngingenakwesaba, (I will go without fear)

Ngocasha kuJesu, onguMhlengi wami." (I will hide in Jesus, who is my Savior)[1]

I listened to the words of this song in utter rapture and was transported to a heavenly ecstasy. Not only was the tune divine, but the heavenly inspired lyrics pierced through my spirit, and I knew then how much I needed the Lord's name as my ticket to heaven. This song brought hope to the hopeless, courage to the fearful, and strength to the weak. I was all those. My family was all that. With my whole family now having found Jesus Christ as our savior, my joy was complete.

My father had been the last family member to give his life to Christ and yet the most impactful. His drinking came to an abrupt end, and his life took a different turn. He could not stop smoking, but the love he got supported him.

A new dawn opened on the horizon and ushered a new hope and a new life. A new journey lay ahead.

My hero traveled with Preacher SaBenon to attend the Christmas convention in Gweru, one of the cities in Zim-

---

1 Hymn #43, Icilongo Levangeli. Published by The Mission Press, P.O. Box 37088, Overport, 4067. South Africa.

babwe, where the Assemblies of God church had gathered. We looked forward to his coming and giving us a report of the convention. He came back a changed man! He tells us that he had smoked a cigarette just before the service, and then he went out to smoke again. He says as he was lighting a matchstick to smoke, he could not bring himself to light it, especially the fact that he was within a church vicinity. He tried again for the second time, and still, he could not bring himself to light the cigarette. He quit. Just like that!

A celebration of my hero was in order. He had quit drinking first, and while quitting smoking had taken longer, he had finally done it. He had been the last person in the family to fully dedicate himself to Jesus, but his doing it brought so much joy to the family and Preacher SaBenon. His complexion started to change from brick red to a nice light complexion. He started gaining some bit of weight and getting stronger.

To us and those close to him, my hero was a living testimony of God's grace. It took him to get out of his family to an unknown land, remote, only to find salvation. As a hero, a police officer, he had saved many, but no one could save him. He could not save himself either. God did. God found him in his weakest state when nothing was going his way, and He gave him a new life. His life was a testimony to what God could do.

My mother was deep in ancestral worship, but once she heard about a God greater than all gods, her life took a complete U-turn, a three hundred and sixty-degree turn. This revolution showed that no matter how deep one is into sin, God's love is greater than the deepest sin.

A church comprised of my family, SaBenon's family, Mkhakhisi Nkomo's family, the Ngwenya family, and NaNjabulo from the Msalili village was birthed. We built an *umshasha* (a shack) to house us for our Sunday service, weather permitting. We would meet in homes if the weather was not permitting. Pastors and guest speakers came from the cities and nearby villages to visit this young yet strong church and conducted inspiring services. A young Pastor Rodgers was dispatched to the Sukwe assembly in 1976 after the Easter Holidays. He was tasked with growing the church while Preacher SaBenon would move to different areas as a church planter. We were also visited by a group of preachers who were preaching about the end times, prophesying of great locusts with scorpion tails that would come and devour the world. To us, this message prophesied difficult times that lay ahead. I remember how scared I was on hearing the message and how I wanted to make sure I remained faithful. Both Preacher SaBenon and Pastor Rodgers saw to our spiritual growth.

Front row: Preacher SaBenon (holding Bible); his two sons on his right Mehlokazulu and Benon; Thompson squatting.

Seated: MaNdlovu, Mother, and Dad.

Third row (standing): Albert (Thompson's young brother), Thobekile (hiding behind Albert), NaBenon (holding baby), my sister Thando, me (standing next to Dad).

Back: Pastor Rodgers Dube, Cousin David, and my brother Shepherd. (August, 1977)

A water baptism followed our conversion. We all made our way to Sukwe Dam for baptism with water. My entire family got baptized that day, and it was one of the most important days of my life. My family's trajectory had changed, and we knew that our journey was only beginning. Now with God on our side, we trusted Him to guide and guard us.

At this point, the War of Liberation was also gaining momentum, but we were being shielded from it. We were tucked away in some remote village.

Part II: The Making

Chapter 10

The Recruitment

During the middle of 1976, the political scene was beginning to deepen and extend its roots among the youth in our rural Gwanda. We could hear of young people who would have tried to cross the Shashe River (Shashi River) into Botswana to join the struggle for Zimbabwe's independence. Some were successful, while others had been caught and jailed or killed.

There were young people in my area who had tried crossing and were caught and put under house arrest. Some had tried several times and had finally managed to cross over to Botswana. To my soon-to-be eleven-year-old brain, I had found this scenario difficult to grasp at the time. I could not understand why anyone would leave his or her family (particularly their mother) to follow someone. The bond I shared with my mother made this difficult for me to fathom. The crossing brought attention to this otherwise remote area. As the "winds of change" were finally reaching this otherwise remote area, they brought anxiety, fear, and uncertainty to our community.

The beginning of 1977 ushered a political awakening of a great magnitude. I was doing my sixth grade at Sukwe Primary School at the time, and since I was born in December, I had just turned eleven. I had started school in January as a sixth grader when Griffin, my classmate whose uncle was a ZAPU rural official, broke to us some unexpected news. We heard that Manama Mission students, faculty, staff, and nurses from Manama Hospital had been recruited (*babuthiwe*) by members of the ZIPRA armed forces to join the liberation struggle.

Three ZIPRA combatants had gathered information about the school through some locals who had wanted to join the struggle. While students were gathered at assembly in the evening, the guerrillas had emerged and led over four hundred students, teachers, staff, and nurses from Manama Hospital to neighboring Botswana to join the armed struggle. The group had crossed the Thuli and Shashe rivers over to Botswana so they would eventually receive training in Zambia as combatants.

The news had sent shockwaves throughout the entire country and the world. This was the first of such large recruitment involving children from the southern part of the country. I went home in shock and delivered the news to my parents. My mother sank down in horror, confusion, and sorrow. We did not know what the recruitment meant. We knew that people crossed the Botswana border willingly, and mostly young adults, not school children. My family was thrown into chaos and confusion. We had not expected the recruitment to involve young children. Two of my sisters were in Manama at the time. Thando was thirteen years old, and Fortune (Nhlanhla) was fifteen years old. Thando had just started her Form Two, while Nhlanhla had just started her Form One. Although Nhlanhla was older, she was a year behind Thando because she had repeated her seventh grade due to her previous poor grade seven results.

A week or so later, my father was called to Gwanda to meet with other parents whose children had been recruited too. A resolution had been made by the then government to bring back the children that had been recruited. The then government of Rhodesia had collaborated with the Red Cross, the UNICEF, the United Nations, the Botswana government, and the ZAPU administration to bring the children back to their home country. Loads of buses filled with parents and families were sent to Botswana to bring back the children. My father was one of the families that went to Botswana to bring his children back. Since no one knew what lay ahead, my sister Fortune and some of my older relatives who had also been recruited, insisted and encouraged Thando, who was thirteen years at the time, to return home as part of the forty-eight children who returned.

A few days later, my father was back but with one child, Thando. It was a reunion with sadness, not knowing if or when we would ever see my sister Nhlanhla again. Thando came home and narrated the story of their recruitment. They had traveled overnight to cross the Shashe River into Botswana. She had sustained severe injuries on both legs while walking. The wounds had left significant scars on her legs. Since there were no other high schools around, my father sent my sister to live with relatives in Bulawayo. She continued with her schooling in Bulawayo.

The 1977 April-May and August-September school holidays were the most difficult for my family, as we had to deal with the unknown political atmosphere. We did not know how Nhlanhla was doing, where she was, or if she was still alive. She had struggled with the curse of tonsillitis all her life, just like the rest of the brood, and we had wondered how she would survive. We did not know where the political climate would take us or leave us. All we could do was pray and trust in God.

The situation began to climax as we could hear of people being killed by either the ZIPRA forces, the Rhodesian army, or a group known as Selous Scouts. Selous Scouts were a notorious counter-insurgency special forces unit that supported the Rhodesian Army. By infiltrating the Black majority population, they would collect intelligence on insurgents. They were reputable for their brutality and were responsible for attacking civilians. They marauded as ZIPRA or guerillas, as they were called. They would gain information and then pounce on the unsuspecting and kill them or have them killed or arrested. They terrorized the villagers. One day we heard that Selous Scouts had killed Mr. Pindi, a local business owner in our village. The news of his death was chilling. We knew that life was never going to be the same again.

One day, the Rhodesian army visited our primary school and gave us a speech about the ZIPRA army, who they had branded as terrorists. The Rhodesian army comprised mostly of White soldiers and a few Black ones. Since this was a remote village, some children were seeing White people for the first time. Seeing soldiers in combat uniforms and wielding guns was quite a spectacle and an experience for most children. It was an interesting visit. We were given beautiful pens as tokens and told to never think of crossing the border into Botswana in support of the ZAPU party.

To deter us from ever supporting "terrorists," as they called those who did not support the White minority rule, we were sent to the river for a shooting demonstration. My sister Thando had told me the difference between the Rhodesian army and the ZIPRA forces. I noted the shape of their magazine, as my sister had told me. A shooting demonstration of a target in the dry river was conducted. We could hear gunshots and were terrified to the core.

I had lived at Ross Camp and had seen White people and White policemen. I had never been terrified of them. Ironically, I was afraid of White children. My experiences at Ross Camp had instilled fear and mistrust of White children. I could not understand why they treated us with disrespect. My mother and I's visit to her aunt NaNtamba who worked as a maid for a White family, also made me fear White people as we were made to stand off at a designated place for Black people. I would admire their beautiful homes at a distance and yet be paralyzed with fear. Dogs would be unleashed on us if we dared get closer. My fear of German shepherd dogs started then and has never gotten any better. I did not understand what was happening at the time. But seeing an army and witnessing what they could do to a "terrorist" (freedom fighters) brought back those memories and gave me a different perspective. I started making the connection.

It was after the visit by the Rhodesian army that children in my sixth-grade class started talking politics. It was then that we heard that Jobe (Job), my classmate Griffin's uncle, who was a Zimbabwe African People's Union (ZAPU) official, recruited people to join the party. We were told not to discuss this information in public for fear of retribution by the ruling government at the time. It was during this time that I heard of the two national parties fighting against the Rhodesian minority rule, the Zimbabwe People's Revolutionary Army (ZIPRA) and the Zimbabwe African National Liberation Army (ZANLA). Although I could not fully understand the implications of the war, I was beginning to realize its reality, and that scared me.

Students started whispering about ZAPU's leader Joshua Mqabuko Nyongola Nkomo. I did not know who Joshua Nkomo was and why he had such an influence on young people to cause them to want to follow him. Boys would talk of going to Zambia and becoming soldiers and then coming back to recruit us. It was inspiring and scary at the same time. Instead of deterring us from joining ZAPU and the ZIPRA forces, the Rhodesian army had opened a floodgate for most people in my area to join the ZIPRA army. We began to hear more about the battles between ZIPRA and the Rhodesian army in Matabeleland and the Midlands area.

My mother's cousin, Bhuzhwa (Bourgeoisie), who had been recruited with the Manama group, would be heard on Radio Zambia calling for all able-bodied people to come and join the struggle. We would lower the volume as we would gather to listen to her. It was unbelievable. A wildfire had been lit and could not be stopped! The ominous storm was finally reaching the remotest villages.

By the mid-1977, a curfew had been imposed in our rural Gwanda area by the then government. We had to be home by six pm. We used buckets at night for relieving ourselves. I was home with Mother, my brother Shepherd, Pastor Rodgers, and Thompson, our neighbor who lived with us. To help my mother with chores, I had to fetch water from the river by myself. I was afraid of meeting any one of the masquerading forces, be it the ZIPRA army, the Rhodesian army, or the Selous Scouts. At that time, the British South Africa Police (BSAP) had unleashed its horseback riding unit to patrol our area. Occasionally they would be seen patrolling our area, and fear of a clash between them, and the guerillas was real. At night we would see lights on our Lote hill, and we would know that the Rhodesian Army were announcing their presence. Since we walked more than three miles to school, we made it a point that we walked as a group. If Griffin and Thobekile were not at school, I would walk the last mile alone. This always gave me chills because the road cut through a bush. It would feel like there was someone watching. It was an unsettling experience.

Meanwhile, big brother, now a qualified teacher employed at Mtandawenhema in the Gwaranyemba area, was fully aware of the political situation. He had been conscientized while attending the United College of Education. He had been preparing his application papers so he could travel by train to Botswana, then into Zambia in the pretext of going to further his education at the University of Botswana. Mr. Cephas Msipa, a ZAPU official responsible for education at the time, was involved in arranging the trip for big brother. Big brother traveled to Harare (then Salisbury) to complete the process. When time finally came for him to travel, his passport had expired. He could not afford to apply for another one as this would have alerted the

Rhodesian government of his plan. The plan to cross the border that way was then aborted.

As children and adults throughout Gwanda were being conscientized about the struggle for independence, more and more of them were leaving the country to join the liberation struggle. Two of my father's sisters, NaRani and NaEnathi, were married and living in the Magedleni area of Gwanda. NaRani's family, Toffee, Dan, and Finn, crossed into Botswana and joined the struggle. NaEnathi's son Enathi also joined his cousins.

My Sengezane family was not exempt from this excursion. With Edward Mbahwa Ndlovu, a high-ranking ZAPU official from this place, having paved the way, this area was already immersed in politics. Edward Mbahwa later represented Gwanda South as a Member of Parliament (MP) after Zimbabwe's independence.

In April 1977, certain individuals at Sengezane met with guerillas and organized recruitment. A day was set for the recruits to meet at the soccer field, where the local soccer team, Tuli Shumbas, played. This team was sponsored by the local grocery store owner, Stanley Noble. Before the game was over, the guerrillas appeared from nowhere and commanded everyone to follow their lead.

My uncles Mpande and James, Patrick, and Cousin Anna's husband Dennis were among this group of recruits. This group crossed Thuli and Shashe into Botswana.

My cousin Charge decided to go hunting with SaKhelina one afternoon. While in the bush, he suddenly heard SaKhelina calling him. He turned and headed in SaKhelina's direction, hoping for a catch. Two steps were enough to come face to face with three fully armed guerillas. He was told not to say a word but to go home and prepare for his recruitment that night. Shivering in his pants, he headed home and could not even manage to eat *indlubu* (round nuts) prepared by my notorious aunt NaPhetsheya. Since the belief was that guerillas could hear everything and could appear and disappear into thin air, he never said a word regarding their presence.

My cousin Nothani was doing his secondary education (Form Two) at Matopo at the time of the soccer recruitment. A few months later, he came home for the August-September holidays. One day, he decided to spend the evening with our cousin Charge at our aunt NaPhetsheya's homestead. While they were eating, a greeting to announce one's presence was heard, and they responded to it by meeting the "'visitors'" outside. Three men in combat uniform showed up and introduced themselves as *"abafana,"* the boys, as guerillas were commonly known. They told them they were recruiting people so they could join the liberation struggle. My cousin Nothani had tried to get out of the recruitment by saying that he was a student. They had dismissed that excuse and told him that they wanted school children so they could attend school out of the country. Nothani and cousin Charge obliged and left Aunt NaPhetsheya in shock and fear. Cousin Elliot was left behind due to his intellectual challenges.

Several homes were visited that night, and many of my relatives were recruited that night. The most interesting recruitment is the one made at Pius' home. Since Sengezane was a place of parties, the guerillas found a group of people at a party at Pius' homestead. They recruited them all, including my cousins Nzathu and Musa. Those who were already drunk, quickly sobered as the shock of seeing the "boys" overwhelmed them. By the end of the night, the group of about four hundred people had crossed the great Thuli River. Three days later, they were in Botswana.

It seemed like it was a matter of time before we could experience the recruitment. My prayer was to be found ready when or if that day came. I prayed to be found with enough clothing to cover my body for the long journey.

Mostly, I prayed to be found with my shoes on because I could not imagine walking barefoot. I had never been to the border, but I knew it was not nearby.

Chapter 11

The Crossing

One Friday, the 30th of September 1977, stands out as a day that changed my life forever. There are very few days in my life that I remember both the day and the date. This one stands out as one of those few. After school, my mother and I had brought my cousin Refiloe (Ree) for the weekend. My sister Thando had stayed with Ree's family two years earlier while doing her seventh grade. They lived close to the school in the Msalili Village. It was customary for Ree to spend time with us, and I would spend time with her family too. So, that Friday was no different. We brought her home for the weekend. Since there was a curfew, we could not stay up till late. By six in the evening, we had eaten dinner and were retiring for the night. My brother Shepherd, Pastor Rodgers, and Thompson used the hut that was adjacent to the kitchen. The girls' bedroom was connected to my parents' bedroom. Mother had suggested that we sleep in their bedroom, but we had turned the suggestion down for that weekend. Since it was a girls' weekend sleepover, Ree and I had wanted to talk into the night. Normally, during this curfew period, I would sleep in my parents' bedroom for fear I might get abducted at night.

This night was like no other. It was an eerie night. The occasional barking of faraway dogs broke the silence of the night. Our dogs responded with a howl that gave me the chills and made my hair stand on end. I wondered what the dogs were seeing or feeling. In my culture, there are several reasons dogs may be howling at night. The howling of dogs at night has been associated with a bad omen, an indication that witches and wizards may be trying to find their way into one's home. The dogs may howl because they may be seeing an unseen spirit. Dogs may also howl as a long-distance communication or to protect their territory. Since the moon was full, the howling could also mean that the dogs were dazed by it.

I listened to this howling and shuddered. I wondered which of the several reasons could be associated with this howling. Due to the political situation at the time, I wondered if the dogs were seeing any of the three mentioned fighting forces, the ZIPRA army, the Rhodesian army, or the Sellout Scouts, or simply howling at a full moon. I felt unease. Ree and I stopped talking and wondered. We could not sleep due to the continued howling. The howling suddenly stopped, and instead of feeling relieved, I felt my hair stand on end. A frightful, terrible silence ripped through the air. Ree and I covered our heads with our blankets, hoping to hide from whatever monster was outside. My heart was in my throat. I felt it in my bones that this was going to be a night to reckon with.

I heard some heavy footsteps approaching our bedroom, then stopped right by my bedroom door. I could not hide under the blankets any longer. I sat up and held my blanket tightly over my chest. I opened my eyes in the darkness and wished I could see through the door. I wanted Ree and me to somehow hide under the bed, but I was paralyzed with fear. I could not move. I hoped none of us would make any sound. The terrible silence was broken at last by the sound of stealthy footsteps and hushed voices. Soft whispers outside alerted me to trouble. The next thing I heard was a soft tap on my parents' bedroom door. Just then, I heard a male voice in low tones commanding my father to open the door and come out. He complied. They commanded my mother to stay put and not move out of her bed. While I was still trying to process all this commotion, a soft knock ripped through my bedroom door, and a harsh commanding voice ordered us to get out of the hut.

Shaking like a leaf, I panicked and got out of bed. And since the mud hut did not have lights to flicker, I looked for my clothes in total darkness. I quickly found and put on my blue cotton skirt and blouse that my sister Orpha had made for me as part of her home economics assignment. Since I had only two pairs of panties, I had washed them that night and left them to dry. In my dazed state of mind, I could not even find my panties in the darkness. We quickly got out of our bedroom to be met with my dad, my brother Shepherd, Thompson (our neighbor who lived with us), and Pastor Rodgers (our pastor) standing in the shadow, surrounded by three armed men. My mouth dried, and I shook to the core. One of the armed men asked if I wanted to get any clothing items from my parents' bedroom. Grateful for the opportunity, I went straight to my parents' bedroom, found my tennis shoes, and wore them. The wardrobe was opened, and I could see my green jersey (sweater), but I was so shaken that I could not even take a step further to retrieve it. I retreated and threw a quick glance at my mother, who had been told not to move.

"Themba kuJesu, mntanami." (Trust in Jesus, my daughter.) Mother was able to whisper those encouraging words to me, and I caught them as I was exiting the door.

I joined the rest of the family outside without my jersey (sweater) and my panties.

"Old man, if you have money, you can give it to your children now and bid them farewell," one of the armed men had said.

My hero went back into his bedroom and brought five dollars and gave it to my brother so he could keep it for our future needs. He bade us farewell as commanded,

"Yah, kulungile. Lihambe kahle." (Yes, it is well. Have a safe journey).

Those were the last words I heard from my hero as he bade the five of us farewell. No one responded. I did not know how to respond. I could not hug him in the threatening presence of an AK-47 rifle. I was numb. My mother had not been given a chance to bid us farewell. My parents' youngest child, an eleven-year-old, was leaving them to an unknown destination. I could not fathom what my parents were going through. I could not imagine what my mother was feeling. I was her world. Only God could give her the strength she needed.

We left our homestead and marched toward the main gate with one of our "captors" leading the way, the second one on our left-hand side and the third one at the rear end. We strode out of the gate in utter silence except for the occasional heavy crunch of gravel and dry leaves made by our footsteps. With a full moon in view, we could see each other clearly and the road to the next village. We left Preacher SaBenon's home to our left and headed straight to Mkhakhisi's homestead. This was a large homestead with several young men. We hid behind a bush, under a shade, while one of our "captors" entered the homestead. Doors were kicked open if a command to open the door was not followed, and people were commanded to get out. Someone seemed to have firsthand information about the sleeping arrangements of each family member. Each hut visited produced a family member to recruit. More than five family members from the Mkhakhisi homestead were taken.

The next homestead was SaS'manga's. We entered this homestead as if we were the owners. I had never visited SaS'manga's homestead because of the vicious dogs. That night it was as if the dogs never existed. They were silenced somehow. We were commanded to stay under the shadow of one of the big huts while the "captors" were invading each hut. I observed this process in bewilderment. Several young men lived in this homestead. Since this was a large homestead, there were many doors to kick open and many people to remove within a limited time.

After what looked like a lifetime, more than five able-bodied males and a girl my age, Thobekile, were taken. While I was watching this process unfold, my dazed brain started to function, and I took it upon myself to check which of the three forces were our "captors." Was it the ZIPRA, the Rhodesian army, or the Selous Scouts? Thando had told me that the ZIPRA boys used AK-47s with a crescent-shaped magazine. I had seen the oblong-shaped magazine used by the Rhodesian army. From my vantage point, I could clearly see the magazine type. I knew at that point that the day I had feared the most had finally come. With adrenaline pumping, I refused to think of anything else besides survival.

I woke up from my wandering thoughts when the command to leave SaS'manga's homestead was issued. We walked to the fourth homestead, and the same procedure was carried out. This process continued until every single homestead in Lote village (except Preacher SaBenon's) had been entered and searched. Some people were being kicked out of their huts, while others were being forced to remain at home.

After every homestead at Lote village had been pe-
rused, and every able-bodied child, youth, and adult had
been located, we were all silently marched to some rocky
place at the edge of Lote. We stopped for a lecture. Our
"captors" introduced themselves as guerillas, *amalwa
ecatsha* (those who fight in hiding), *abafana* (the boys),
and freedom fighters under Zimbabwe People's Revolutionary Army (ZIPRA), which was the Zimbabwe African
People's Union (ZAPU) army wing. I had already identified them by their crescent-shaped magazine and their
camouflage. Being able to identify my "captors" had given
me some relief. I knew who they were, the ZIPRA army
guerillas, affectionately known as the "boys." I relaxed,
knowing that we were in the hands of the ZIPRA army
than Sellout Scouts or the Rhodesian army.

The guerillas wore a plain green camouflage combat
uniform and covered their heads with similar caps. With
trousers tucked into their boots, they were ready for war.
The commander, as we got to know him, hung his Light
Machine Gun (LMG) over his shoulder, and rounds of
bullet ammunition crisscrossed over his chest. He was a
no-nonsense man who looked confident and composed. He
gave his orders once, and they had to be obeyed. We were
told to lie down if we heard sounds of gunshots. We had

to differentiate the sounds made by the ZIPRA army guns and that made by the Rhodesian guns. We were also told to differentiate between their AK magazines and those of the Rhodesian Army. Theirs was crescent-shaped, whereas the Rhodesian army carried an oblong-shaped magazine. I took all this in and got into survival mode. There was no turning back; I had to survive whatever this ordeal meant.

Once everyone had been accounted for, we continued our journey. We walked under the gaze of the full African moon in total silence. The only sound to be heard was that of heavy footsteps and an occasional corking of the gun. The night was calm yet tormenting. The beautiful blue African night sky, with its dazzling milky way, had turned into a nightmare. After several hours of walking, we arrived in Shanyawugwe, our neighboring area. We entered a thick dark forest with tall trees and a carpet of tall wet grass. We were each told to find a dark spot where we could hide from the bright moonlight and rest before the journey ahead. It was here that we met as a conglomeration of Sukwe, Lote, Nkalange, Silonga, Buvuma, and Kwete villages. The Buvuma group had looted Mathayi store and other stores in the Buvuma area and was carrying the supplies.

In the hustle and bustle of finding a resting spot, I had lost Ree and friends Alice (Ally), Sikhanyiso, and Sukoluhle (Suku). Since we were not allowed to move about for security reasons, I identified a small shrub and sat by it. Just as my eyes were beginning to droop, I felt something like a drizzle on my arms. In the wink of an eye, it had started to rain. As if the heavens were cleaning evidence of our footprints, it started to pour. It was that kind of rain that comes from nowhere and drenches the whole place without warning. The silent rain drenched me within a short space of time. I crawled my soaking body to a different location, under a big tree. I slumped my exhausted body and faced the opposite direction of the rain. No matter what location or position, I got drenched all the same. Without a sweater, I started feeling the cold rain prickling like thorns on my bare flesh. I shivered from fear, anxiety, exhaustion, and cold. After what seemed like an eternity, the rain stopped.

Finding a dry spot was a nonstarter, so I slumped my exhausted body on the grass and used a nearby shrub as my pillow. Exhausted as I was from walking, I tossed and turned on the grass to find comfort and warmth. I eventually closed my eyes and prayed a short prayer to ask God for protection. Before I could say, "Amen," my heavy eyelids had voluntarily closed. The rain had brought with it some cold air, and the night had become viciously cold. I froze with every minute of my sleep. Wet grass would not allow me to seize a moment of peace. I tossed and turned on my wet grass bed and could not keep warm. A deep sleep finally visited me in the early hours of Saturday and took me out of my fear, anxiety, and exhaustion into my warm bed in my bedroom. I had found some reprieve.

I woke up with a start at the sound of a distant cock-a-doodle-do, to see a sea of people laying down like frozen timber at the mercy of a lumberjack. Having walked half the night, this sorry sight told a story of great sacrifice, pain, and suffering that lay ahead. It was now Saturday, the first day of October 1977. One of the "boys" was calling us to get moving so we could be out of the thicket before daybreak. I woke my frozen body and mind and looked for familiar faces I had lost during the night. All I could see was a multitude; an estimate of over two hundred people would not be an exaggeration. And among the multitude were the Sukwe primary school teachers, including the "destroyer" and the headmaster, Mr. Cephas Sibanda. It was a sight!

We proceeded south toward John Deep, where we met a group from Mkhalipe. We rested and were served food. We sat down in groups and were told to wait our turn. I was already dehydrated and suffering from a sore throat. *Isitshwala (pap/sadza/ugali)* and boiled beef were served in large washing dishes to feed the multitude. We were seated based on age groups. As the food was being lowered to the ground, I saw children in my group getting the food while the dishes were still being lowered to the ground. By the time the dishes had been lowered, there was nothing left to eat. I had managed to grab only a full hand of *isitshwala* and no meat at all. I had tried to eat the i*sitshwala* that was in my hand, but I could not. I had developed a sore throat. I did not know when the next meal would be provided. I had not grown up as a hassler; I was used to being taken care of. Not only was I the only one who could not eat due to a sore throat, I could see Ree crying. She, too, could not eat, and she had resorted to crying. This scenario left me confounded and hungry.

After John Deep, we crossed the main road that led to Hwali and headed toward Siboza area. To cross the road without being detected by the Rhodesian army was a challenge. Branches were put on the road, and we had to walk on branches facing the opposite direction, giving the impression that we were on the other side. The last person had to clean up after we had all crossed. We reached Siboza, a hilly area, and rested. This was the last recruiting place. Here we met groups from Hwali and Mnyabetsi.

The guerillas, now as many as twenty or thirty, were drinking and playing loud music. They had managed to recruit as many as over four hundred children and adults without being detected by the Rhodesian army. They had every reason to celebrate. Over twenty villages had become a war zone. While I needed to rest, I was also nervous. Even as an eleven-year-old girl, I did not think that drinking and playing loud music at that time was responsible behavior. I wondered what would happen if the Rhodesian Army descended on us. It was scary to imagine. I trusted the "boys," just like everyone. I still remember one of the songs they played and sang nonstop. One of the guerillas we got to know as Huzo (pseudonym) would hold his Light Machine Gun (LMG) as if playing guitar. He would sing along with a song from their cassette player, *"We-e ntombi yami yekel' ubugebenga."* (Oh, my girl, stop being a criminal.)

The last recruiting stop.

Later, towards the evening, we were given food. A cow had been slaughtered, and *isitshwala* was prepared. Food was served on corrugated iron sheets. This time I had learned my lesson. As soon as the food was brought down, I reached out before the iron sheets were set on the ground. I was able to get at least two handfuls of *isitshwala* and one piece of meat. I could not eat it due to tonsillitis. Ree sat there and cried again. Tears were just running down her cheeks. She could not eat either due to tonsillitis.

Later that day, we went into a village where we retired. This village had a large *isiza* (threshing floor) we used to retire. As I was trying to find a sleeping place, I saw Israel, one of our village boys, and asked him for his sweater. He willingly removed his only sweater and lent it to me. It was then that I felt warmth and slept well for the first time.

The following day, Sunday the second of October 1977, was one of the worst days of my life. We were woken up very early in the morning because we had to make it across the Zimbabwe/Botswana border that day. Keeping and feeding us on the Zimbabwean side was a challenge both logistically and defensively. We were a multitude. We had to cross the two big rivers, Thuli and Shashe, to make it into Botswana. The Thuli River is a major tributary of Shashe River, while Shashe River is a major tributary of the Limpopo River, which borders the southern part of Zimbabwe and the northern part of South Africa. Crossing these two wide rivers would expose us since the rivers were an open space.

After walking a few miles, we reached the great Thuli River. We crossed the Thuli River closer to the Thuli irrigation. We had to run across the river at full speed. The river was not too wide to cross at full speed. Although we had not had any food at this time, it was still early in the morning to gunner sufficient energy left from the previous night to run across the river. After crossing the Thuli River, we continued walking, now heading to the Shashe River.

It was still early in the day on Sunday when we finally reached the border. We sat down and hid under the bushes while our recruiters cut the border wire so we could walk across. We were given a lecture while other "boys" were scouting the area for security. We were told to run across the river and never lag. Whoever lagged would be shot as he or she would pose a security risk. A signal was given to allow us to get into the Shashe's dry river sand. Children were commanded to cross first. I got into the dry river with other children and trotted for a while. Halfway through the dry river, I gave up and started walking. I could hear adults passing me by and encouraging me to run while others were cursing and yelling at me. Some were pushing me out of their way.

With a sore throat, tonsillitis, a headache, hunger, and exhaustion, I could not take one more step further. I was weak and tired. I gave up on life and did not care if I was shot or not. I told myself that whoever wanted to shoot me, let that person have a good day. I continued walking at a very slow pace while others were passing me by. I heard the yelling, but I simply did not care. I am one of those people who does not give up on life easily. I fall and rise because I know that life happens. There are only two times in my life where I was faced with a life and death situation, and I gave up on life. This is one of them. Now, I knew I was at the tail end, and I still did not care. My feet started to get heavier, and I was feeling dizzy; lifting each foot became laborious. My tennis shoes were filling with sand as I took each step forward.

There were few people at the time who were still trying to run across the dry river sand, given the fact that we were a multitude. Among the few who were lagging was Daisy, my village neighbor. A large thorn had pricked her barefoot, and she could hardly walk. I knew she was behind me.

I was among the few who could pose a security risk to the recruits. As I was about to stop moving and stand still right in the middle of the great river Shashe for a shooting demonstration and death to take me, I felt four strong hands grabbing my arms and lifting me up. One of the "boys" carried me on his back and ran with me across the river. He put me down under a shade. I was given sweets (candy) and water to drink. Once I identified where Alice and my friends Ree, Sikhanyiso, and Sukoluhle were sitting, I walked over and slumped down and leaned against Alice's shoulder. I was in Botswana with the rest of the recruits. I had survived. I had made the crossing, and I was glad the ordeal was over. Or was it?

Chapter 12

The Kalahari

Resting under the bushes by the Shashi Riverbank, I could not believe I had safely crossed over to the Botswana border. Exhausted, relieved, and anxious, I closed my eyelids to catch a break. My throat, throbbing and burning, would not allow me to even swallow my own saliva. All I could feel were pins and needles firing from my throat and out through my ears. Tonsils! I was in trouble. Our last meal had been the previous day in the afternoon. Even then, I had struggled to eat even one gulp of *isitshwala (pap/sadza/ugali)*. I was hungry, and all I could think of was food and rest. I hoped we were not far from our destination. While we were waiting for everyone to join us, I closed my eyes just for a second to catch a break.

"Everyone up! Let's go, let's go!" We had barely rested when a call to get going was made.

As soon as we emerged from the bushes surrounding the Shashe banks, we heard a shout of *"Lala phansi!"* (Take cover!). Those were words from the guerillas. We scurried and found a few bushes to hide.

A Rhodesian spotter plane had found us and was flying high above our heads. It was a scary experience. We stayed under the few bushes in hope that the spotter plane would not spot us. We heard a voice in a loudspeaker from the Rhodesian spotter plane above us saying to us, *"Phendukani!"* (Go back!) We took cover and stayed under the bushes along the Shashe River for a while. Those who were wearing brightly colored or white clothing were commanded by the guerrillas to remove them or turn them inside out to avoid being detected by the Rhodesian spotter plane.

After some time, seeing that the spotter plane had disappeared, we came out of hiding and continued our journey inland. There was no extra clothing for those who had had to remove their clothing. We emerged from the bushes with naked children, men, and women! Some women and girls had had to remove their bright-colored or white tops or dresses and were walking with their breasts uncovered. Some men had to remove their trousers or shorts and walk in their underwear. We had people who were half-naked! No one cared at this point! It was later that we found time to laugh about it. We were all in a survival mode. This time, we followed a dry riverbed where there was some cover, and we walked along it for a while.

The spotter plane was back and hovered over our heads for hours. We would walk, run, and hide and walk, run, and hide for miles while the spotter plane hovered over our heads. It was an intimidation game and a dangerous one.

After hours of following us, the spotter plane finally retreated, much to our relief. Maybe seeing little children such as my eleven-year-old self and others deterred them from bombarding. Or the possibility of being in the Batswana territory may have deterred them from making a bombardment. Had the person(s) in that spotter plane decided to call for jets and helicopters to make a bombardment, that could have been a massacre of great magnitude. Tired, hungry, and thirsty as we were, we would have perished in great numbers. Survivors would have been devoured by the unforgiving desert that lay ahead. It is a mystery why they never called for a bombardment. One can only believe that God prevented it. He did not allow it to happen. God protected us that day.

After surviving the deadly game with the Rhodesian spotter plane, our journey westward towards the inland and through the vicious Kalahari became more treacherous and laborious. The vast uninhabited treeless landscape emerged before us and issued severe warnings ahead. Few scattered drought-resistant trees and shrubbery stood amiss as far as the eye could see. A forest of acacia also spread out and fiercely guarded this vast landscape. The red sandy soil with thorny shrubs proclaimed a message of hopelessness. The barren semi-arid inhospitable landscape viciously welcomed us, the sojourners, with its harsh sunlight.

With each excruciating step, the savage heat ravaged us and baked us into charcoal. Judging by the sun's position, given that we did not have watches, the sun stood still slightly above my forehead. It was around mid-day, and the temperatures were already soring. With temperatures soaring to as high as 110 degrees F (43-46 degrees C), we were drenched in sweat and burned through our ripped clothing. Dragging every footstep and dreading this endless vicious desert heat, I soldiered on. Every step became a difficult effort. My body ached from head to toe.

There was no water in sight. The desert stood up to its Tswana name, which is derived from the Setswana word Kgala, meaning "the great thirst," or Kgalagadi, meaning "a waterless place." The roads shimmered in the heat of the midday sun. I could see the gleaming white surfaces ahead, and a hope of a sip of water would be raised, only to be quelled by the realization that the shimmering white surfaces were some salt pans. These salt pans were a result of some soluble calcium minerals and salts caused by the evaporating water. My heart would sink as the desert heat continued to descend on my burned, exhausted, and dehydrated body. With each stretch of this endless dry landscape, all hope of water would be lost. I dragged my swollen feet and began to wonder if I would survive this ordeal.

It was late in the afternoon when we eventually bumped onto some water. A stream of water was running down from a hill. We scrambled for water and kneeled to sip. As I was kneeling to sip, I saw that the water had some green covering caused by frogs. I scooped it away and tried to drink. Oh, the pain! I could not drink the water. My throat was in excruciating pain. I was dehydrated and had a sore throat. I tried drinking again, thinking that it would be better the second time around. My throat and chest were on fire! It felt like there were needles and pins in my throat and chest. I persevered and drank the water through the most excruciating pain I had ever experienced in my life. Tears just ran down my cheeks uncontrollably. As our journey continued, we would struggle finding water, and if we did, we would struggle drinking it.

As we continued our journey through this desert land, we realized that we had lost our headmaster, Mr. Cephas Sibanda. We could not find him. We reported the situation to the combatants. We suspected that we had left him behind where we had last rested. Each time we rested, most of us would fall asleep. We would be awakened from our slumber by the issue of a command from the combatants to start moving. It was advisable to have someone close by to wake you up.

Pastor Rodgers, who was asthmatic, was also struggling to breathe. The area we were passing through had been set on fire, and the smoke and dust from our feet were making breathing difficult. I also kept checking on my brother Shepherd.

It was later in the afternoon that we started to see scattered villages. We passed through Mabolwe, *emlageni*, a place where villagers fed cattle during the dry season. Just as the sun was about to set, we arrived at Gobojango, our first destination. Since Botswana's policy prohibited freedom fighters from using her territory as a base, the "boys" quickly disarmed and changed into civilian clothing and mingled with us. It was then that some of them were identified by those who knew them. The two guerillas who had carried me across the Shashe River in my weakest moment came over to ask how I was.

The guerilla who had masterminded this great mission was also identified. He had worn a cap so low that it had covered his face most of the time. He had talked little for fear of being identified. Their mission had been accomplished. It was one of the greatest and most dangerous recruiting endeavors of all time. They had successfully recruited over four hundred individuals, children, and adults from over twenty villages in one attempt!

The reason for taking children was strategic, we later learned. The ZAPU party had wanted to bring to attention the plight of the Africans in then Rhodesia. By taking children to be part of the struggle, they had wanted to share with the world the impact of the Rhodesian Bush War on children and adults alike. Schools were going to close, and that would have an economic impact on the ruling Rhodesian government.

As I sat down in relief, I looked at myself and refused to play a pity party. My cotton skirt resembled *isitshikitsha* (traditional dancing skirt made with dried grass). It was tattered and torn. My tennis shoes, although new at the time of my departure from home, had developed significant holes in them. The soles had been eroded, and sand was finding its way into the shoes. My feet were swollen; they resembled that of a baby elephant. I had scars all over my legs that had been unleashed by the thorny shrubs that characterized the landscape that I had walked past. My notorious hair had had a hay day! Kinky as it was, it looked like dry grass on sandy brown soil and felt like iron brush. With hollow and blood-shot eyes due to exhaustion, I looked like a ghost.

I could not help but wonder at what I had been through. I had made the crossing, survived the spotter plane war game with the Rhodesian army, and my body had carried me through the vicious waterless Kalahari Desert plains. We had traveled from Friday night to Sunday evening and had covered more than eighty kilometers (about fifty miles) as the crow flies, which could be double the distance on foot since we did not use a straight route. Others had covered more, depending on their starting point.

There was no time to feel sorry for myself. I had to grow up. The same God who had determined my every move, seen me through my life, would carry me through what lay ahead. He already knew what lay ahead and the impact it would have on my life and others. I was already a warrior.

I remembered my mother's words as I left her lying in bed that Friday night.

"Themba kuJesu, mntanami." (Trust in Jesus, my daughter).

My mother's last words meant the world to me. "Trust in Jesus, my daughter." She had said as I exited the hut. Although we were not a perfect family, we were close-knit and loved and cared for one another. We had shared both commemorative and challenging situations as a family. I valued my extended family, my village, and my support system for giving me a strong foundation and preparing me for a future that lay ahead. They had given me love, and I banked on that love to keep me strong, whatever situation lay ahead. Although I had been plugged from that support system, I was grateful for having had them in my life. Thinking about them and valuing them would carry me through whatever lay ahead. Armed with an everlasting gift of love from my family and village, I knew I had been prepared for the future. I felt strong and refused to succumb to depression.

My mother had named me well. I was the Guarded One, *uLindiwe.*

Chapter 13

The Refugee

After having conquered the gruesome Kalahari Desert into Gobojango, we rested for a little while before being loaded into trucks by the Botswana Defense Force (BDF) for our next destination, Bobonong. As we were being loaded into those trucks, we were made to sit in the trucks with open legs so the next person could sit right between those legs. This was an embarrassing and degrading experience. I realized then that I was then a refugee, and I had relinquished most, if not all my rights, that is, if I had them in the first place. We traveled at night to avoid detection by Rhodesian security agents who were operating in Botswana.

We spent that Sunday night in Bobonong, which was a police camp. Our headmaster, Mr. Cephas Sibanda, was found and joined us. Having reported him missing, a helicopter and the Botswana Defense Force had been sent to scout the area. He had followed us alone, crossed the Shashi River, and met the vicious Kalahari Desert. He had found a water source with reeds and had survived by eating those roots. In fear of being devoured by animals, he had climbed a tree and stayed there until morning. Hearing a cock crowing, he had followed the sound and was led to *emlageni* (one of the cattle grazing areas). It was there that he was rescued and later joined us. His is a story of survival against all odds.

The following day, we were divided into groups and registered our names for records. We were registered as refugees. My status had changed from that of a simple citizen to that of a Rhodesian refugee. Here, we were able to walk and meet Tswana families by the water tap. We could not go further than the demarcated place.

I was still struggling to eat. At this point, I could not drink or eat. Since the group's numbers had dwindled, I could take my time trying to force myself to eat.

The following day, on Tuesday the fourth of October, we left very early in the morning for Selibe-Phikwe (commonly known as Phikwe). Selibe-Phikwe was originally a female prison that had been turned into a refugee camp. Female prisoners were housed on the opposite side of the camp. It was one of the two transit centers that accommodated asylum seekers at the time. The other transit center was Francistown. By ten o'clock in the morning, we were registering and being prepared for our life as refugees in Selibe-Phikwe. We went through the screening process by immigration officers who asked the reasons for our leaving the country. At this point, I had a very good reason, in which my reply was,

"I would like to go to school in Zambia." Obviously, one genius had fed me with that response. It was a standard answer. It worked.

We were sent to the tents to receive some health supplies, clothing, and blankets. With two light blankets in hand, we were led to our hostel. Ree and I shared a double-deck single bed, with Ree using the top one while I used the bottom one.

I met many people in Selibe-Phikwe who had either been there before me or arrived after me. It was in one of the tents that I met Sihle and Sheilla from my Sengezane village. They immediately took me under their wings. Sihle had been my sister Nhlanhla's childhood best friend. One day, as I was lining for food, lo and behold, I saw Nothani with cousin Charge. They had been recruited a month or so earlier than me. I had last seen them more than three years earlier when we relocated to Sukwe. Although we were meeting under different circumstances, it was a welcome reunion.

In less than a month after we had left Sukwe, Preacher SaBenon had followed. He had left behind a young wife with three children, all below the age of six. It was through him that I got an update on my family's whereabouts. The night of our recruitment, Emmanuel had waited for the bus to take him home for the weekend. The bus never came. Apparently, the bus driver had been tipped about the impending recruitment. Had the bus come, he would have been recruited with us. He had spent the whole week without knowing the fate of his family. When he was able to get on the bus the following weekend, he found an empty home. With my dolls laying at the back of the house, and our livestock laying in the yard, he feared the worst. With a disheartened heart, he went to the neighbor's homestead, who recounted the details of what had happened to my family and the village.

Threats against my father were issued by one villager. He worked with Selous Scouts to brand my father as a sellout since he was an ex-policeman and had several of his children out of the country to join the liberation movement. Selous Scouts infiltrated the villages and pretended to support the nationalist movement while gaining information. They had already killed one of the businessmen in the area. I was recruited with my friend Sifiso and her three siblings. Her father owned a store in one of the neighboring villages. While the children were in Zambia as refugees, someone branded their father as a sellout. Selous Scouts came, burned down his store, and killed him. Many villagers suffered this fate, especially if they were successful. A concerned villager heard about the threat issued against my father and alerted him. My parents upped and left for Gwanda and later moved to Bulawayo, where it had all begun.

Selibe-Phikwe housed both males and females. ZAPU recruits included both males and females, while other parties did not have female counterparts. There was a demarcation that separated male housing from female housing. On Christmas and New Year's Day, we mingled and visited our male relatives. This was called *"emahlangeni,"* like letting the cattle graze in a harvested farm area. It posed a security risk, but we were grateful for the opportunity. My brother had been in the same camp as me, but we could not see each other that often. I was able to see him before he was shipped to Zambia for training. That day, we met in SaBenon's barrack and conducted a service. So many of us who had been recruited from Sukwe were able to meet in Preacher SaBenon's barrack and conduct a service. By the end of the year, most of the males I knew had been flown to Zambia for training.

Recruits from different liberation movements that were fighting against the minority rule in Zimbabwe could be found here at Selibe-Phikwe. The majority were ZAPU recruits. Different groups had a way of identifying themselves from the rest. Some shaved their hair on the sides and left a mohawk, while others shaved off their hair and left goatees to set them apart. Some wore all black, while others combined black with red or with green. Some looked like hard-core criminals. Different languages were spoken, an indication of the cultural and ethnic diversity of the peoples of Zimbabwe. Although different ethnic and language groups and liberation movements were represented here, each had one purpose in mind, to liberate Zimbabwe from a minority rule.

I have always struggled with toilets. Toilets in Selibe-Phikwe were a challenge too. They were constantly blocked and always produced a stench that I found revolting. With the number of recruits living at the camp, the toilets could not hold up. It was a health hazard.

Our food was cooked outside, and we lined up for food outside. The food was different from what I was used to. We ate something that was yellow and was cooked in the form of thick porridge. My friends and I have never been able to determine what it was. Others think it was cassava. We also ate *isitshwala* (pap/sadza/polenta/ugali) made with yellow cornmeal. Most of us had never seen or eaten yellow cornmeal. It was novel. We also ate canned sardines, which we liked a lot.

My worst nightmare was oats. First, I had never eaten or seen oats. We ate oats for breakfast almost every day. My heart would sink at the sight of it. This oatmeal would have weevils in it to show that the consignment would have taken a long time to get to the refugees or would have been stored for a while before being used. When cooked, the oatmeal would be slimy, and I would struggle to eat it. Given that I struggled to eat okra due to its slimy nature, I could not eat oats either. It being slimy and infested with weevils, I found it revolting. Most of the time, I would skip breakfast for that reason. I could not be given anything else. I was a beggar; I could not choose. Although the choices were limited, the food was good and appreciated. While my friends and I would complain about the food, we would also appreciate its availability as we were told about the different donors.

I had "celebrated" my twelfth birthday at the end of 1977 as a refugee. The beginning of the year, in 1978, ushered new hopes of going to Zambia to start schooling. We had been in Phikwe for three months. While waiting for our final move to Zambia, we had tried to keep ourselves occupied. The camp was small and crowded, and there was hardly any form of entertainment available. We woke up and did some basic training, showered, went for breakfast, lunch, supper, and back to our barrack.

Butsang (sister to Ree) was selected as the lady on duty. She would organize teams to play netball (like basketball) with the locals in Phikwe. Supporters could accompany the team. One day I went to Phikwe as our team supporter and came back only to find my friends Sukoluhle, Sikhanyiso, Sifiso, and Ally (Alice) missing from the barrack. I was greeted with messages from other girls saying that the commander had been looking for me so I could travel to Zambia with my age mates. I was devastated. I had missed my chance to travel to Zambia, so I could go to school there. I had told the immigration officer the reason for my seeking asylum was so I could go to school in Zambia; now, my chance had been derailed simply because of a netball game! I could not believe it. I climbed onto my bed to cry and feel sorry for myself. All my friends had left! Disappointed and unhappy with myself for the decision I had taken, I decided against feeling sorry for having gone to play netball. I reported my presence to the personnel in charge of traveling. Her response was interesting,

"We have been looking for you everywhere!" she yelled. Records showed that I had gone for netball. But since we were never told when we would be leaving for Zambia, we were supposed to be always ready. I was caught unawares and had missed my flight.

"You are scheduled to travel to Zambia today. We need a Maphosa on the list of those going to Zambia today. You have to get ready to leave this evening."

That a Maphosa was needed to travel that day puzzled me, I did not know what it meant. All I could deduce was that maybe since we had traveled as a group, my last name was missing from the children's list that had traveled in the morning. Whatever that meant, I was ecstatic! Although I was going to travel with adult women, I was glad for the second chance. I was the only young girl in that group to travel that evening. Since I had nothing, I did not have to spend time packing. No bag to pack. With plaited hair, I was good to go. My first time flying! My almost spoiled day became the best day ever.

Chapter 14

The Induction

I had just turned twelve years old when I experienced flying for the first time. It was now January 1978. My flight from Francistown to Lusaka in Zambia had been short and exhilarating. The few bumps did not matter to me. I had been told that airplanes bump when they fly above high mountains and a big river. So, I assumed we were flying over those mountains and over the great Zambezi River, which runs along the Zimbabwe, Botswana, Namibia, and Zambia borders. All I could think of was being able to go to school. I had been out of school for the whole third term, that is, from September to December of 1977. I was going to be part of those children who were going to open the first-ever ZAPU girls' primary and secondary school at Victory Camp (VC) in Zambia. This was going to go down in history! Life was going to be good, and before long, our country would be free, and we would be reunited with our families. Maybe in six months... Maybe by the end of the year... Soon... Soon... I was sure. I hoped.

I could not contain my excitement as we landed in Lusaka. I sat in the airplane, waiting for the next command. Just as I was still deep in my thoughts, we were told to exit the airplane and follow the lead. Since it was already the evening, I could not see my surrounding; all I could see were lights at the airport and on the distant horizon. We went into the vacant airport where we were processed and then sent to wait at a quiet and dimly lit corner. The atmosphere at the airport put me on edge. There seemed to be some urgency and secrecy among those who were responsible for us. I went from ecstasy to anxiety and concern within a short period of time.

We exited the airport building toward our military vehicle in military style, a single formation. At the command of "Quick! Quick! Quick!" we scurried into the truck and sat down quietly. The vehicle was covered and would not allow for sightseeing. Since it was already in the evening, I was content with that. The driver started the vehicle, and I could feel my stomach knotting. I wondered at what lay ahead. I held on as the vehicle maneuvered through the dusty road from Lusaka, the capital city of Zambia, to my destination.

We stopped at what I assumed to be the gate at Victory

Camp, my would-be home, hopefully for a short time before Zimbabwe attained its independence. The truck driver turned off the engine and the lights. I could hear muffled voices outside, and suddenly, a bright light shone in the truck and on to our faces. Having checked the truck and its consignment, the guard at the entrance gate allowed us into the camp. Our driver started the engine without turning on the lights. We drove in darkness, under the moonlight and headed to our final stop. How the driver could see the road in darkness baffled me. It was as if our presence would alert an enemy lurking in the vicinity. The whole camp was in total darkness except for one dimly lit house. An eerie feeling settled over me, and I shivered as my knees rattled and gave way under my body. I did not know what to think of this welcome.

We were sent to the dimly lit house, where we were welcomed by several male and female guerrillas. Among the group was a short, stocky, and dark military man. With a bold head and a clean-shaven face, he presented a confident persona. His snake-like eyes pierced through the room, penetrating the soul like a sharp knife. It was as if he had powers to read the mind. His stout and hairy arms spoke of a valiant man who had stood and survived the test of time. Here was a military man, a guerilla welcoming us to this camp. He stood confidently in his full military gear, with his gun hanging on his left shoulder.

Although I felt intimidated by his presence, I also found myself fascinated and drawn to him in reverence. He was a formidable force to reckon with. He greeted us with a commanding voice that thundered and sent chills down my spine. He introduced himself as Cecil, the camp commander.

"Hello, comrades. This is Victory Camp. It's not your mother's kitchen. You hear me? If you are here as a Selous Scout, know for sure that you will follow the fate of others. You may not know what happened to them, but you will know soon. We do not fool around here. First things first!"

These words of welcome cut me in the gut, and I shook to the core. What kind of welcome was this? I wondered to myself. I thought I was coming to school; I did not realize that I had come to a war zone. Being addressed as "comrades" took me by surprise as we had used the word to refer to the guerillas. This camp presented a different vibe, that of war. I was scared.

There were also female combatants. I had never seen women in combat uniform before. I looked at them in admiration. Their presence took me back to the beginning of

1977, when I had last seen my sister Nhlanhla. She had in-dicated to my father her desire to proceed to Zambia so she could train as a liberation fighter as part of the ZIPRA forc-es. She had asked my sister Thando to return home with our dad since no one knew what lay ahead. As I looked at these brave women, I wondered about my sister Nhlan-hla's whereabouts. I wondered if they knew her.

The military girls took over as commanded, and we were each taken to a private room where we underwent a thorough body search in case we were part of the sellout group, the Selous Scouts. We were asked many questions to ensure we knew where we were and the reasons. I re-sponded to the questions as honestly as I could.

Having passed the test, we were sent back to the wel-come room.

"This is a war zone, comrades. We are at constant threat of being attacked. There is no time for stupidity here, as you can put yourself and others at risk. You hear me? You follow orders here. There is no "I." We are in this together. We live together, and we die together. You hear me?"

A briefing regarding camp policies and the political structure was conducted. We were told about security risks in the camp. Many Selous Scouts had been picked up inside and outside the Victory Camp while trying to infiltrate the camp and attack it. Our camp was at risk of being attacked by the Rhodesian Army at any time. We lived under perpetual threat from our enemies. We had to be always vigilant. We learned about different communication codes. We had to master what each signal meant, where to hide, when to run, and when to hide. The briefing had emphasized the importance of following orders to avoid compromising the security of others. Following the right channel of command was important for our survival, we were told. For that, we were introduced to the leadership and their responsibilities at the camp.

The briefing also emphasized the need to live together in harmony, not as different ethnic groups. There were many ethnic groups in the camp since ZAPU was a multi-ethnic party. We were told there were no Ndebeles, Sothos, Vendas, Kalangas, Shonas, or Tongas; we were all Zimbabweans with one agenda, to liberate our country. We were *"Abantwana Benhlabathi"* (Children of the Soil) fighting for the liberation of our country. Our unity was important in winning the war.

"Anyone heard being tribalistic would be severely punished," we were warned.

As I sat there, taking this information in, my body shook with fear and apprehension. I could feel my heart in my throat. My knees wobbled. My stomach knotted in fear. I was gripped with fear. Fear. Fear. Fear. Fear of being attacked. Fear of being bombarded. Fear of never going back to my homeland. Fear of how long the war of liberation would last. Fear of the unknown. I shuddered.

"No time to feel sorry for yourselves here, comrades. Too late for that! You hear me? Here, we are all going to be soldiers- in heart, mind, brain, and body. You hear me?"

One of the military personnel, a young woman of about twenty-five years of age, bellowed as she locked her eyes with mine. Had she read my mind? I wondered.

My young brain could not comprehend all this information. I could have cried and said, "I want my mommy!" but I knew better. I knew at that time that I was morphing into a young warrior. I knew I would have had to do what it took to survive. My desire to survive drove me to follow orders and do whatever it took to avoid putting others at risk. It was not about me, but it was about others. I was being taught to put others first.

The last part was to change our birth names to pseud-onyms. I was given a new name and assumed a new identity. My name was a simple ordinary name. I did not find it exciting, so I did not encourage its use. Some people I got to know at the camp had fancy names like Kajongwe (a cockerel), Country girl, English, Zambezi, Lizard, Juju, Kunzima (tough situation), or Bourgeoisie. And besides, I had had many nicknames growing up; I found an additional name not necessary.

We were given light blankets and spent our first night in that house. We slept in whatever we were wearing, including our snickers. In case we had to run away from the camp, being fully clothed would help. Darkness enveloped my heart. Fear gripped me, and my mind kept playing the "being-attacked" game. I could not sleep.

I woke up with a start as I heard the blowing of a whistle, a code for us to wake up and go to parade. One of the female guards woke us up by kicking our feet. The whistle continued blowing at certain intervals until everyone was assembled at the parade. We formed a single file and followed our leader to the parade. The female guard led us to the parade and ensured we were paraded with the right company. The group I had traveled with joined the last company. It was a company of adults who helped in the camp in various positions. It also included medical personnel and teachers for the school that was to open soon. I was the only child in that company since I had traveled with adults.

I was met with a sea of people, young and old. This group was much larger than the one in Botswana by far. There were thousands of us, including children much younger than me. The parade was organized into companies, platoons, and sections. About nine to ten people formed a section, three sections formed a platoon, while four platoons formed a company.

As we paraded, a convoy of about five or so cars suddenly made a grand entrance and parked by the parade. Some officials and military personnel hurriedly got out of their cars and moved to different strategic places surrounding the cars. Others moved to various positions around the parade. Some of them quickly started to make their way toward the parade. Black and White officials exited the cars and came toward the parade. It looked like an important person was in the house. It was a spectacular military display.

A group of people from the convoy made their way to the parade. I had no clue who they were. To me, they all looked trained and professional. Some were in full ZIP-

RA combatant gear, while others were dressed in civilian clothing. One individual stood out to me. He was big built compared to the rest. He carried a knobkerrie. He was in full ZIPRA camouflage, including a matching cap. He was surrounded by people who had come with him, each seeking to defend him with their lives. I looked at this display of loyalty in amazement. As he was approaching our parade, our camp commander and his personnel saluted him. He talked to our camp commander and his staff first. Our camp commander turned to face us and issued a command.

"Comp...a...knees! Atte...n...sheen!" (Companies, attention!) bellowed our camp commander.

"Hah!" came our response.

We had taken basic training at Selibe-Phikwe, and we knew what it meant to stand at attention and at ease, and we knew how to do it as commanded. In unison, and with shoulders pulled back, chest out, and hands by our side, we quickly lifted our right knees and stomped our right feet to the ground. We stood at attention as had been commanded.

"Stand...a...tease!" (Stand at ease!). For that, we relaxed and separated our feet. He repeated the command again until he was sure we were all attentive and ready for the guests.

"Atte…n …sheen!"

"Hah!" we responded again.

"Sa…lute!" (Salute) came the command.

At that command, we saluted and then stood at ease as commanded.

"Today, we welcome our uMdala (Old Man) to our camp. Let us sing a welcome song for him."

Our camp commander made the announcement in our isiNdebele language.

Wait a minute! Our very own national activist and leader of the ZAPU party was here at our camp to visit us. His Excellency, Joshua Mqabuko Nyongola Nkomo, was right there before my eyes. It was an incredible and exhilarating experience that I could not even describe. My only hero had been my father. I had not grown up idolizing people. There were no celebrities that I could idolize and follow their every move. I lived in villages, and there had been little information about anyone. Here I was in the presence of greatness, in the presence of the man I had come to revere and idolize. I was mesmerized by his presence. As a twelve-year-old, this first encounter with the ZAPU leader was unprecedented. My eyes were deceiving me.

He was affectionately known as *uMdala*, meaning the old man. This address carries with it dignity and respect of an elderly person. Culturally, an elderly person is revered for his knowledge and experience in life, hence the name uMdala. He was known as *uMdala Welizwe*, the old man for Zimbabwe, or *uMdala Wethu* (Our Old Man). For security reasons, his visits were normally never announced to the camp. We had not been told that he was going to pay us a visit.

As requested, one person started a song, and everyone took it up with vigor and sang at the top of their voices. A beautiful harmony was heard rising and wringing throughout the parade, bringing hope of an independent Zimbabwe through this great stalwart leader.

> *"UNkomo wethu somlandela*, (We will follow our leader Joshua Nkomo)
>
> *Nkomo* (Mr. Nkomo)
>
> *Somlandela, somlandela*, (We will follow him)
>
> *Yen' uNkomo wethu."* (Our leader Joshua Nkomo)

At the end of the song, this revolutionary leader approached the parade with a beautiful smile on his face. He raised his knobkerrie and uttered the slogan that we had grown familiar with. His voice, much smaller than his physique, could be heard rising with emotion.

"Ziiii!" he raised his knobkerrie with his right hand.

The parade erupted and responded to the slogan by raising their right hand diagonally as if cutting the air.

"Zimbabwe!" came the response.

"Zimbabwe!" the speaker raised his knobkerrie.

"Ziii!" the parade erupted.

"One Zimbabwe!"

"One nation!" we responded.

"One nation!"

"One Zimbabwe!" we responded.

After this slogan, uMdala, the ZAPU leader, talked for a while about the school and the buildings that were already taking place and introduced some White guests that had accompanied him to officially see where the school would be built. Some were taking pictures while the guests spoke. This charismatic speaker offered hope of an end of the war. I was drawn to his speech; I was uplifted. I could envision our country's liberation in a few months.

"We are not fighting against a race or an ethnic or tribal group. Remember that we are fighting against an oppressive rule perpetrated by the Rhodesian minority-ruled government. We are fighting against an ideology meant to suppress the majority rule of the Black people in their country. And we will win."

Then towards the end of his speech, he asked,

"Are you hungry?"

"Noooooo! Yeeeees!" came the two conflicting responses.

Just a handful from one company had responded with a yes, while the rest of the companies had responded with a resounding no. This response infuriated uMdala. He was visibly upset. He addressed the camp first.

"It upsets me to hear that you are hungry. There is plenty of food that is sent to feed you. Do not hesitate or be afraid to let your commanders know when you are hungry. They will let me know. Something has to change because I do not want you to be hungry."

He turned to the camp officials and talked to them before bidding us farewell with words of encouragement and another slogan.

"We will be independent very soon. Right? Do not be disheartened *Bantwana Benhlabathi* (Children of the soil). He concluded his speech.

"Ilizwe!" (The country!)

"Ngelethu!" (Is ours!) responded the camp.

"Ngelethu!" (It is ours!) he raised his knobkerrie.

"Ilizwe!" (The country!) erupted the camp.

As the convoy left, our camp commander addressed us, reminding us how important it was to follow rules to keep us safe. Soon after his speech, one of the female combatants, a military security guard, addressed us and ordered the company that had reported being hungry to come forward. She called them out by their company name.

"Whoever reported to uMdala (the Oldman) that you are hungry, come forward. Be ready! You know yourselves." When no one dared to surrender her life to this fire-spitting guerilla, she moved forward and identified the company by its letter identification.

"Comp...any! Atte...n ...sheen! For...war ...d ... march!" (Company! Attention! Forward march!)

That company marched forward as commanded.

"Down, everyone! Crawl! Roll! Exercise number nine right now! Run! There is no playing here. Fools! You think we are playing here! Fools!"

I shook down to the core! What was happening? Before I knew it, this company that had reported being hungry was being punished. They were crawling and rolling and jogging at the order of their commander. They were bathed in dust from head to toe. Others had been dipped in a mud puddle and resembled tadpoles.

After the punishment was over, they joined us at parade in their muddy and dusty outfits. It was a sight! Not all of them had responded with a yes, but they had suffered the consequences brought upon by a few of their company members.

"Comp…a …knees! Atte…n …sheen!" (Companies! Attention!)

"Hah!"

"Stand…a…tease!" (Stand at ease!)

"Hah!"

"If you have a problem, you do not report it directly to uMdala! You hear me? There is nothing wrong with reporting that you are hungry. It is the protocol that needs to be followed, and you know the right protocol. Do not be fools here! We do not want confusion here. Who do you think you are? Fools! You are in a war zone. Get that right into your foolish minds right now!" yelled one of the commanders as she spat balls of fire and venom.

My mouth went dry. My knees shook. Since we hadn't had our first meal of the day, I understood why the individuals could have responded the way they did. I was hungry too. However, protocols were considered important if we were to survive through this ordeal. We were all supposed to be in one accord. Seeing the company dressed in dust and mud and spitting grass, dust, and pebbles gave me a clear picture of where I was and who I would become in the time ahead. I went through a roller coaster of emotions within a few minutes, from ecstasy to melancholy.

By the end of my first week, I had a pretty much good idea of the camp surroundings, procedures, and my purpose. I had been inducted into the system.

Chapter 15

The Parade

The parade was where everything happened. It was an open space that accommodated thousands of people. We paraded for various reasons. First, parade was a way of taking attendance. As discussed earlier, we were grouped into sections, platoons, and companies. Although I had first come with a group of adults and was placed in their company, I was moved to one of the first companies since I was among the youngest. This group was known as *"okijana,"* derived from the word kids. At parade, we commemorated special events and faced disturbing incidents.

Since there were many of us, eating took the whole day. We paraded so we could easily and orderly line for food, based on our companies. Since I was in the first company, it meant that we were the first ones to eat. One day I paraded late because I was on cleaning duty with a few roommates. By the time we got to parade, everyone was standing at attention. I was coming from the opposite side of my company. I had managed to maneuver close to the middle of the parade. For fear of retribution, I just stood behind one company with the hope that I would run to my company as soon as they were standing at ease. I found myself being the youngest and shortest in that company for the second time. The only person I knew in this company was Melitha. Although she was three grades behind me, she was three years older and much taller. I stood behind her towering body, and all I could see were the backs of other girls' heads. There seemed to be no chance of making my move to my company, as we were kept at attention for a while. Commanders were making inspection rounds.

Just as I was trying to plot my escape route, one of the female combatants who knew me came to this company and commanded us to stand at attention. I started panicking for fear she would notice that I was in the wrong company. To make matters worse, I was standing right at the back. Short as I was, it was obvious that I did not belong there. I was a misfit. We locked eyes, and I prayed I would not be a demonstration. I could not imagine doing exercise number nine and the embarrassment it would cause. Although it was still in the morning, I could feel a rivulet of sweat running down my spine. I knew it was over. I was toast!

She addressed us as she stealthily and pompously walked between the sections toward me. I was paralyzed with fear. At that point, I knew I would be a demonstration; there was no way out. All I could think of was exercise number nine. The next thing I heard was,

"Lindi! You will be the platoon commander!"

"What? No, please, I can't. Please!" I begged.

I hoped she had not heard the "no" part and only heard the begging part, since orders were to be taken without question. She pulled me by my hand and sent me right in front of the platoon. I was declared the platoon commander of about thirty older children! I did not even belong to that company! I did not even know most of them. These kids had been to VC longer than I had; they knew better. It was unbelievable. I was petrified. I wanted to cry. I had grown up with a family of leaders; leading was not my forte. I did not see myself as a leader. I did not want to be one. I was used to being taken care of, not the other way around. And that's the world I preferred. My being a platoon leader of this company meant eating later, whereas in my *okijana* (kids) company, we ate first. This meant I would have to call out "Atte…n…sheen!" and change my voice to sound like a commander. That was too much for me. I just felt depressed there and then.

With knees shaking and voice quaking, I pulled myself

together and took on the challenge. I called for attention and followed the protocol when it was time for us to line up to eat. I went through the process like a robot and convinced myself that I was going to try to forget this ordeal.

The following day, that company had to find another platoon commander. I had deserted and demoted myself to a simple *kijana*. I had gone back to my original *kijana* company. I had told a few close friends about my saga, and they had sympathized, although some had envied the position. I had spent a sleepless night tossing and turning, and I was not going to allow that situation to control me. I planned. My hero was not there to protect me; I had to stand up for myself. I had so much on my plate. Although this self-demotion and desertion was a violation, I was prepared for the worse.

Since we wore similar clothing, I was going to blend in with other *kijanas* in my company, and no one would identify me. So, I thought. Just as I was standing in parade, fully blended with other *kijanas*, I saw the female combatant talking to my commander. I was mortified. They had both looked at me and laughed. I did not know what that laughter had signified. I did not know if the problem had ended or I was in a worse situation. I did not know what would happen to me next.

Later that afternoon, I visited the combatant in her tent to resolve this issue. It was eating me up.

"Hey, it's Lindi, the Platoon commander!" She made the announcement and greeted me cheerfully.

"Yes, about that… I cannot do it. Please." Lowering my voice to ensure no one heard, I pleaded my case and explained the reason I had been in that company in the first place. At that point, I knew that punishment was inevitable but better than being a platoon commander.

"Now, you have been officially released from your duty! Okay."

Before I could say a big thank you, she proceeded to give me a lecture,

"Let me ask you something. How do you think commanders are identified? You think it's magic? No. Being a leader is not about age. It is mental stamina. You hear me? You can do it; it is just that you are telling yourself that you are younger than those girls and not yet mentally ready. You did well, though. Well done!"

Hah! I did well? I could not believe what she was saying. I still do not know whether my promotion was punishment for being in the wrong company or it was a real promotion and a mere coincidence. All I knew at the time was that I had to do something to deal with the problem that was threatening my mental health. I was prepared to even plead my case to the camp commander but knew how important protocol was; I had to face her and plead my case. I knew my limits.

At parade, we also welcomed guests like the ZAPU leader, Joshua Mqabuko Nkomo, and his high-ranking officials such as Joseph Msika, Willie Masarurwa, Thenjiwe Lesabe, John Nkomo, Stephen Nkomo, Edward Mbahwa, the ZIPRA commander Alfred Nikita Mangena, and organizations like the United Nations High Commission for Refugees (UNHCR). It was the speeches of such leaders and supporters that gave us hope for a bright future in a free and independent Zimbabwe. To welcome guests and respond to their messages of hope, we would respond by singing and uttering slogans that kept us hopeful.

Issues would be addressed at assembly. Divisions among combatants and those who had completed their secondary education and were bound for further education were reported. The ZAPU leader, Joshua Nkomo, would use the parade to address such issues as arose. Issues of tribalism were addressed there and then. We were all "children of the soil," not Ndebeles, Shonas, Khalangas, Sothos, or whatnot. One of his great reconciliatory speeches he uttered showcased him as a great leader, a unifier and is recalled by many residents at Victory Camp.

"My children, we fight in different ways. Some fight using guns, others through education, cooking, sewing, and so forth. We all have different skills and need to appreciate each other's strength and know that we are doing this to build a future Zimbabwe that would have all skills."

At parade, I got to experience basic military training. The officers would segment a word where it would not otherwise be segmented, and the word would sound completely different from its original meaning. They would segment and prolong the syllables for about five or so seconds before completing the word. They would put an emphasis on some syllables and draw in some air on others. It was possible to end up not knowing that the words were in the English language.

"Comp...a ...knees! Atte...n ...sheen!" (Companies, attention)

"Hah!" would be our response.

"Comp…a …knees! Stand…a …tease! (Companies, stand at ease)

"Hah!"

"Comp…a…knees! Atte…n …sheen!"

"Hah!"

"Comp…a …knees! Sa…lute!" (Companies, salute!)

"Stand…a…tease!"

"Atte…n…sheen!"

"Comp…a …knees!

"On the dabul!" (Double)

"Kurura!"

The word *"kurura"* does not exist in our isiNdebele orthography, so obviously, some genius made it up. Anyway, once the word *"dabul"* (double) was uttered, we knew it meant to make a fist and curl both arms as if using some dumb bells or weights for biceps curls. "Kurura" was a command to start moving.

At parade, we perfected the skill of toy-toying, a high-stepping movement. This movement was accompanied by some nonsensical rhythmic words and phrases.

Our officers would chant something inaudible, or nonsensical, or sometimes a meaningful or coded message, and we would respond.

"Helele itoyi-toyi inamandla. (Toyi-toying is strong)

Umdal' ufun' izinyamazana, (The Old Man wants animals)

Tshuba gijima, nyamazana (run, animal)

Tshuba gijima killer man (run, killer man)

Dolo phezulu nyamazana (high knee, animal)

Dolo phezulu, killer man" (high knee, killer man)

Some people would pass out while toyi-toying. My chest would burn, and I would feel like spitting blood.

The parade was also a place where the commanders would unleash their wrath. We would be commanded to lie down, crawl, roll, and leap like a frog. Leaping like a frog was known as exercise number nine. It was a notorious exercise that gave me nightmares for a long time. We would place our hands behind our heads, squat, and leap like a frog. By the time we got to our designated point, our legs would be wobbling, and we would be walking with a limp. You would see people's tongues out, hyperventilating like a tired dog. With limited resources, we would continue wearing the same clothes and change only if dipped in mud.

We also crawled and rolled. The crawling took a toll on the elbows, and they would look like some skin had been sliced off. None of these exercises were fun. We did them for survival. We understood the constant threat that we faced and that we were supposed to be physically and mentally fit in case we had to run.

The parade ground would unleash its fury in many ways. I would be standing at attention and then feel something moving down my neck or up my leg. Sometimes, something would move about in my hair or fall off my hair. I would desire to scratch, but because I would be standing at attention, I would hold on. Yes, lice. I had never seen lice in my life. It was at the parade that they seemed to be more active.

There were two types of lice, the black one that would wiggle in my hair and sometimes fall off. I would feel them going down my neck and/or my face. Maybe there would be so many that they would be fighting for a better spot. Or maybe they would be overfed and start to fall off. Who knows? It was during a time when I was supposed to be standing at attention that such an exhibit of disrespect would be displayed. There would be brownish-yellowish ones that would climb up my leg during parade and either cause a tickle or a sting. Moving one's limbs while standing at attention was a no, no. This was a nightmare!

During our spare time, my friends and I would squash them with our thumbnails and help each other squash theirs. It would be like watching animals grooming each other! Only that we did not eat the lice like some animals do. The smell would be horrendous. Occasionally my brain would deceive me and bring back memory of that horrendous sight and smell. We did not have shampoo, and our health supplies were limited. Haircuts partly solved the problem. Haircuts!

Chapter 16

The Camp

Our Victory Camp was a holding camp for females, young and old. It had an intimidating military atmosphere at the time of my arrival, early in 1978. It oozed with an eerie feeling so depressing that it would weigh down on my shoulders and engulf my soul. A thick deathly cloud hung over the camp and made my stomach sick with anxiety and fear. With no streetlights and with a curfew, evenings turned into total darkness that could be sliced with a kitchen knife. I would imagine what lurked in and around the camp. As darkness fell, my heart would fail me, and I would be paralyzed with fear. Mornings, although welcome, clouds of uncertainty rose and hung over the camp. Living and surviving at VC required great sacrifice, humility, and resilience. The conditions challenged my mental and physical well-being, and a repertoire of coping strategies had to evolve.

The camp had been a farm inhabited by the People's Movement for the Liberation of Angola (MPLA), who had offered it to ZAPU at the end of their war (Saha, 2012). Few old buildings were dotted around the camp, including three houses and one of the largest ZIPRA armory and the logistics. The armory later became a factory where uniforms and clothing for the *kijanas* (kids) were sewn. The logistics housed our supplies, donated food and clothing. We received donated clothing from all over the world, including the United States of America, Cuba, the Soviet Union (at the time), and the East Germany (GDR at the time).

I will never forget this one dress that some of us *kijanas* (the kids) had. It had long sleeves, and I wore it often since it was the only winter dress I had, among my three dresses. I had had a cholera shot in Botswana, like everyone else. This jab was given on the left arm between the elbow and wrist. For someone who had lived on jabs my whole life, this was an unusual place for a jab. It caused me problems for a long time as it just would not heal. The jab created a visible scar on many people's arms. For me, the jab left a wound that did not heal for over a year. I would be given antibiotic tablets, but they would not work. Many times, yellow and blood-stained puss would ooze out. If I wore this long-sleeved *kijana* dress, it would stick to the wound, and I would have to carefully and painfully remove the scab that would have stuck to the dress. This process bothered me for a long time. It was after having an antibiotic jabbed around that area that the wound finally healed and left a big scar in that area.

Few people occupied the houses. I had been told to find a place to stay. My friend Sikhanyiso had found her aunt, who stayed in one of the houses and had invited me to join them on my second night at the camp. This house was nicknamed the "University," and many teachers lived there. Many people occupied this house, which had several small rooms. The house looked gloomy, casting a shadow of abandonment. The creaky floor and its squeaky door handle spoke of years of use and abuse. It was in this house that I made my abode and joined the crowd to become one of the residents. I could not, however, shake off this dreary feeling.

Behind the houses was the tent city. Hundreds of tents lined up and were home to most of the residents at this camp. Small tents and large tents, all in camouflage green, lined behind the houses. Grass, dust, and pebbles characterized the inside of the tents. Having heard of my presence, my mother's cousin, Sithabile, invited me to stay with her in the tent that she shared with others. I obliged and left the "University" as I could not shake off this dreary feeling. With no beds or mattresses, I would spread my thin blanket on the ground to be met with either the grass, dust, or pebbles. There was no winning. I dreaded each day. Instead of bringing hope, each morning brought with it sadness for what might lie ahead, and the evening darkness brought fear and anxiety.

I was horror-struck when I visited the toilets. Toilets were the most shocking and appalling to me. I have always had a thing with toilets. Ross Camp, Sengezane, Sukwe, and Selibe-Phikwe, and now VC. This was a never-ending saga for me. Two toilets had been dug further down behind the houses. Two long and deep pits had been dug. Logs had been placed across the pits. One had to balance on the logs and squat to relieve oneself. This presented an intimidating situation as I feared falling into the pit. Paralyzed with fear, I watched this death trap for the first time in total shock.

The open-pit toilets also provided no privacy. It was an open space. I had never seen anything like that before. The first time, I could not relieve myself with everyone watching. With little choice to none, I eventually succumbed to this dreadful death trap, like everyone else, and used it as a toilet. It was one of the most degrading experiences in my life. It was this choice or the stream. The pungent stench from the pit toilets would emanate and pollute the air.

There was a stream that always ran with water. It was on the far end of the camp. I would make a beeline to that stream with my friends, Ally and Sikhanyiso. This is the stream that we also used for bathing. I would find a bush by that stream and relieve myself. When it rained, the waste would flow into the stream, the same stream we used for bathing. Since the stream was far from the tents, I knew I would have to get used to the open pit toilets sooner than later. Both the stream and the toilets were a health hazard that, even as a child, I could conclude.

There was no proper kitchen. A shed structure was put in place, so cooking would be done. Such structure posed a challenge during the rainy season. The firewood would be wet and would take longer to light. *Isitshwala* (pap/sadza/ ugali) was cooked in drums, and it would take hours to cook for the whole camp. As a result, we ate most of our food cold most of the time.

We ate once a day as it took the whole day to prepare for a large number of people at the camp. For protein, we would have two or three bean seeds and broth. Most of us knew this bean as a wild bean, *umtshatshatsha* (Acacia tortilis), that was part of goats' diet in Zimbabwe. It could have been any bean, but to us, it resembled goat beans. To us, the bean was unsuitable for human consumption, but we ate it all the same. The problem is that the bean required hours of cooking hence we ate it not fully cooked most of the time. For me, I found the broth more palatable than the bean itself.

Fish was part of our dietary plan and accompanied *isit-shwala* (pap/sadza/ugali) as a side dish. We ate dried fish of all shapes and sizes. We ate boiled and heavily salted and dried mackerel and carpenter fish. Pieces of crabs and snails, and sack threads, collected during the fishing and packaging process, would be cooked as part of the fish. There would be no one or time to separate these unwanted intruders. Having struggled with the smell of fish my life, I met my match with these dried ones and the intruders.

We also ate meat once a week on Thursdays. We would be given one piece of meat and some soup or broth and a large serving of *isitshwala* (papa/sadza/ugali). At first, I learned to be content with the one piece of meat and broth and have those with courage to go for seconds share with me. My friends Ally and Sikhanyiso were professionals in getting seconds without being detected, so I relied on them. One faced severe punishment or a whip by Mdluli if detected.

As time went by, I eventually gathered the courage to go for seconds also without being detected. I learned the skill of eating my meat and broth as soon as it was served and would quickly make a U-turn for a second or third serving. Sometimes I would hide the meat under the *isitshwala* and just extend my plate while hiding my body behind some bodies. I had to do what I had to do. It was difficult for the kitchen staff to keep tags on who would have eaten or not. For that reason, we would spend almost the entire day in the dining hall area on Thursdays. Having a kitchen staff member who knew you was considered a double-edged sword. One could get more pieces of meat from that staff member, or that very person would report you or remove you from the line.

The process of going for a second serving was known as *ukutshaya amawela* (going for seconds or having twins). There were many pros and cons to this behavior. Children, including yours truly, ate first, and they normally would go for seconds and thirds. Because of that, adults who lined up after the children normally would end up without meat. Sometimes they ended up having to wait in line while skimmed milk was being prepared for them. This meant going vegan for the whole week.

Since I had perfected the skill like Ally, I would eat so much meat that my stomach would hurt. Several times I puked in my bed at night due to overeating. Given that the toilets were outside, and I was afraid of going to the toilet at night, I finally came to my senses and decided to eat no more than I could handle. Ally was a well-known *amawela* (second servings) pro who could fill a one-liter container with meat. Since it was one piece of meat per plate, that meant going back about ten times to be able to fill a one-liter container. We would eat the meat for several days and suffer from a stomachache with each consumption. We finally decided to stop the madness by eating what we could handle.

There were many foods that I found difficult to eat. It was later in my adulthood that I began to appreciate the donors who had sacrificed and donated the supplies to us under the United Nations High Commission for Refugees (UNHCR). Officials from the organization would occasionally visit our camp, and so would other donors. We later heard that because we spent so much time at the dining area on Thursdays, it had become the targeted day for an attack by the Rhodesian Army. Someone had leaked the information. That was bad news.

Several groups existed at Victory Camp. Children from birth to sixteen years old, and boys under nine years, were at the camp and were known as *okijana* (small kids). I belonged to that group known as *okijana*. We were the majority at the camp.

OnaKijana (mothers of small children), nursing women, and pregnant women were also at the camp. Children were born at VC, something that was always a mystery to us kids, why and how there were that many pregnancies. Since school-aged children were separated from the adults, we did not understand the situation. Not knowing what the situation was, fortunately, most pregnancies were among adults and not children. One can only hope that whatever situation was, it was consensual.

Other women worked in the kitchen as kitchen staff and chefs. Sis Daisy, our village girl, also helped in the kitchen. Some women worked in the clothing factory as dressmakers. Together with some men who came from the Workers' camp, they made uniforms and other clothing items.

There were also military women who guarded the

camp. They lived in tents with those who were passing through on their way abroad for their training. As children, we would observe many women, trained or untrained, leave camp to further their education. Teachers left to further their education. Children were also sent for cultural exchange programs to other countries.

Like any other environment, there are always social classes. Even at VC, there were those who we considered rich or privileged. We called them *izicupha* (those who scoop, the privileged). They had relatives or significant others in Lusaka, the capital city of Zambia, who would pick them up for the weekend or visit them regularly in the camp. They could afford bed sheets and better clothing. They cooked their own *ingiyazana* (special food), including chicken. Since chicken was never on our menu, this group was privileged enough to include chicken on their menu.

As soon as word got out that I was at VC, I found many relatives who were willing to take care of me or act as my surrogate mothers. Sithabile was my mother's cousin. While leaving at Ross Camp, my mother and I would visit NaNtamba (Sithabile's mother), where she worked as a maid for a White family. I am not sure how Sithabile found me, but she did and took me in so I could stay with her in her tent. She was three years older than me and had been in the camp for a year. She had left Zimbabwe soon after the Manama group at the beginning of 1977.

A whistle would be blown at four o'clock in the morning for us to go for parade. I would jump and get ready to head for parade. Sithabile would continue sleeping and tell me to ignore the whistle. I would be on edge, fearing being punished. She would only go when the combatants would budge into the tent and start beating them up. I found this behavior puzzling. She knew the combatants and took advantage of it. To avoid punishment and "putting everyone at risk" as I had been warned, I would jump at the first sound of the whistle and head for parade. Having grown up with law and order, I would find it difficult to ignore the whistle like Sithabile. I would go to parade with the few who were like me. I would fall asleep at parade while waiting for others to show up. Sithabile would be the last one getting to parade and would evade punishment.

Country girl, my mother's cousin's wife, became my surrogate mother. She was a loving and caring woman. Her husband Kilibone was my mother's first cousin who would visit us in Sengezane from across the great Thuli River.

Country girl had left children and a husband and joined the liberation struggle. Even though I slept in Sithabile's tent, Country girl kept my supplies and clothing.

Victory Camp School opened its doors in February of 1978, as had been promised. The camp atmosphere changed from that of a military camp to that of a school. Dorms, modern toilets, and classrooms had been built by builders from the Workers' Camp. Preacher SaBenon had been one of the builders. He had been sent out of the country to learn the skill. Together with other builders, a beautiful school had been erected. It was a sight to behold. We moved into our dorms and shared single bunk beds in pairs. We still slept fully dressed and in our shoes. Modern toilets to match our dorms were built. We no longer had to go to the bush or use the hideous pit latrine. Although we were children, we still faced perpetual threats. A cloud of uncertainty continued to hang over us.

For the first part of the year, we had learned under the trees. A movable board would be leaned against a tree for the teacher to write on. Before the school was built, we would use whatever building was available to learn. At the time, there were only a few buildings, and the walls would help provide support for the movable boards. Books and school supplies were provided by different donors. With the opening of the school, classes were conducted in classrooms that were fully furnished. School supplies were provided, including furniture. As the year progressed, a large hall (Big Bhawa) was built. It was partitioned to provide more classrooms.

Content at first was more political in nature. We were taught by one of the political commissars. We would learn about the liberation movement, the party structure, and the like. Once the school was opened, we followed the Zimbabwean curriculum so we could not lag. We learned the English language, our isiNdebele language, social studies/ science, and mathematics. It was a fully-fledged curriculum. We wrote the national Grade Seven exams as Zimbabweans did. We were motivated to learn.

The daily morning parade ceased. We did not continue with the exercises and toyi-toyi. We did not have lice anymore that would devour us at parade. We attended assembly instead of parade. At assembly, we were addressed by headmasters and teachers, not commanders. They talked school language about the curriculum, the grades, homework, and school supplies. We welcomed guests at assembly, not parade.

The school was comprised of the primary and secondary levels. The primary and the secondary levels were led by different headmasters. Mr. Matjaka was the secondary headmaster. He had been recruited with the Manama group early in 1977. There were many children at the primary level and fewer female teachers. Once the classrooms were completed, most of us in higher primary grades were taught by male teachers. The secondary level enrolled only the Form Ones (Grade Eight) at the time, as most of the seventeen-year-olds were in training at Mkushi, a training camp for girls.

Teachers were recruited from among the residents. Some were already trained teachers, while others had completed their secondary education, and it was deemed appropriate that they could at least teach elementary. Male teachers volunteered and came from our sister camp J.Z.Moyo Camp, which housed the boys. They taught mostly sixth grade to secondary level. Our Sukwe village primary headmaster, Mr. Cephas Sibanda, and my former Sixth-Grade isiNdebele teacher Mr. Madume Noko were among them. Incredible sacrifice!

Having left Zimbabwe the previous year without completing the year, most of us were not confident about proceeding to the next grade. Although we were two-thirds into the year and a third away from completing our sixth grade, we had not been to school for a whole term. And the next grade level came with national examinations. We were not sure we were ready for the seventh grade. Most children repeated the grade they had last attended. In our group, only Suku proceeded to the seventh grade. She was the brave one, as we called her. She was intelligent, too; we knew she would be fine.

Older women took on positions as surrogate mothers once we moved into the dorms and slept in dorms with us. They were the ones who were tasked with telling us bad news, good news, and taught us how to be girls. NaMusa, from our Sukwe village, became our surrogate mother in the dorm that Ally, Sikhanyiso, Suku, Ree, and I occupied. I still maintained Country girl as another surrogate mother since NaMusa had the whole Sukwe village girls to look after.

One day I was called by my surrogate mother, NaMusa. I got into the dorm and sat on a bed, wondering what news she had for me. I was never a perpetual rule-breaker, so I knew it had nothing to do with rules. She looked somber, and I knew I was going to receive bad news.

"Good afternoon, Lindi," she had greeted me with a forced smile.

"Afternoon, auntie," I responded.

"I called you to let you know that your sister Orpha passed on and was buried two days ago. She went into a diabetic coma and never woke up. Some guerillas who came back from the frontline reported this information so it could be relayed to you."

Just like that! I was stunned! The news shook me to the core. My sister was gone. I loved that girl with all my heart. I had looked up to her. She had a beautiful soul, loving, caring, and kind. I was devasted. I could not imagine my mother at that point.

My knees felt weak. Tears started running down my cheeks. I sobbed heavily. I wanted a private place to moan my sister, but I could not find one. I climbed on my single bed, which I shared with Melita, and cried. I cried for my mother. With three children she did not know if they were alive, now her older daughter was gone. I could not fathom her pain. I cried for my family, for our loss. I cried for myself. With no one to comfort me, I quickly wiped my tears and nose and headed outside to join my friends. I wondered if Fortue and Shepherd would hear or had heard the sad news.

Chapter 17

The Combatants

Since the camp was huge and one could easily stay for days without knowing where others were, it was important for my friends and I to establish a point where we could meet. We had identified a spot close to the parade to make it easy for us to dash to parade when the whistle was blown.

A few days after my arrival, my friends and I were sitting by the spot where we normally conglomerated when we saw our camp commander Cecil headed in our direction. We stole glances at each other, hoping none of us were in trouble. It was usual for him to interact with people and know what was happening in his camp and around. Nothing was beyond his knowledge. He seemed to know everything and everyone. As children, we were drawn to him like a magnet. He was a fatherly and brotherly figure to many of us. We revered and venerated him. For him to be tasked with such a huge responsibility spoke of his character and bravery. He was likable and knew almost everyone in the camp. I had come face to face with him a few days earlier during my induction, although he had not spoken to me directly. So, his coming to us was not anything out of the ordinary. He walked confidently as he approached us.

"How are you, *bokijana*?" (kids) he greeted us cheerfully.

"We are fine," came our response.

After this greeting, the camp commander shifted his gaze to me and smiled.

"How are you, Fortue?"

We looked at each other, puzzled by this greeting. Who was Fortue? Seeing the puzzled look, he asked if my sister's name was Fortune. Oh, Fortune! My sister had gone from Nhlanhla to Fortune for her to repeat seventh grade at Sukwe and move on with her education. So, here she was known as Fortue, a nickname. How the camp commander had linked me with Fortue blew my young civilian mind. Nothing escaped his snake-like eyes and his small ears. He had known who I was from the very first day, and the military girls had known too. I braced myself for news regarding my sister. I had last seen or heard from her a year earlier.

"Yes, I have a sister named Fortune." I had to give

short answers since I did not know where this conversation was headed.

"When was the last time you saw her?" asked the camp commander.

"I last saw her at the beginning of January last year when she went to school at Manama," I responded nervously.

"Well, she sends her regards." Camp Commander Cecil said, smiling from ear to ear.

Those words just did it for me. I held my wide-open mouth in my hands as I took in the news. Although I was supposed to be a little soldier, I could not help feeling emotional. My sister was alive! And someone knew where she was. The news brought hope to my heart. I was telling everyone who cared to listen where my sister was. Who wouldn't?

"She is okay. She is undergoing training." He did not have to say where she was undergoing training, as we both knew where.

That piece of news brought me so much joy that I could not explain. I was a young sister of military personnel. I was so proud of my sister. How the camp commander had linked me to my sister beat me at that time. I felt like someone always knew my whereabouts.

Several of my female relatives passed through VC from their training camps on their way abroad to further their education. It seemed to be the party's norm to have as many as could qualify to further their education abroad. This was done to prepare them for easy transfer of power once the country became independent. Among those was my aunt, my father's cousin, Sikhangezile Juliet Manjala Maphosa. Aunt Sikhangezile had been recruited from the Manama group as she was starting her Form Five (equivalent to Grade Eleven) at the time. She underwent training at Mkushi and had risen to the position of company commander both at V.C and Mkushi. She was sent to Jamaica to further her education. After completion of her studies, she went to Kenya for an advanced secretariat course.

Bourgeoisie (Bhuzhwa), who had been recruited from the Manama group, was my mother's first cousin. She had undergone training at Mkushi and had risen to a position of a Detachment Commissar. This allowed her to recruit on Radio Zambia in Lusaka, broadcasting on Short Wave directed mainly at recruiting from Zimbabwe. She also was tasked with spreading information about the liberation struggle. While still in Zimbabwe, we would lock the door and lower the volume so we could listen to my mother's cousin calling people to join the liberation struggle. She brought consciousness to most young people after Manama recruitment through her announcements on Radio Zambia as she would encourage young people and all able-bodied people to join the war of liberation.

Bourgeoisie (Bhuzhwa) also rose to the Battalion Commissar, charged with running the library, listening to Rhodesian and world news, and disseminating information to the Battalion. At the end of military training, she was sent to Guyana for a course in Secretarial Science. This is when she passed through VC and brought news of my sister Nhlanhla's presence in Mkushi.

My aunt Moratiwa (Mora) Valentine Gazi (aka Abigail Mabetha) was also one of my mother's cousins. She did her training at Mkushi and was identified as one of the first group of fifty combatants to train as military instructors. A few months into being trained as an instructor, the Rhodesian Army attacked Mkushi. Although she survived, she will never forget that day, just like most of us. She tells of how it all went down on the day of the bombardment.

I had uncles, too, who were trained personnel. Some of

them would frequent VC for various missions. One of my maternal uncles was driver and security personnel for the ZAPU leader, Joshua Mqabuko Nkomo. His brother was one of the camp commanders. My uncle Ben Diliza Maphosa was high command, responsible for Victory Camp (VC). I would occasionally see them during their missions, and they would give me hope of the war's ending.

"My niece, you will be okay. Do not worry; we will be free soon." My uncle Ben would say these words each time he was at VC. Those words always gave me hope.

I considered myself lucky to have my uncle in such proximity. He would bring me bread, and I must confess, I did not always share with my friends. Sometimes I would go behind the dormitory and eat it by myself. I would sometimes put it under my pillow and keep eating a little bit at a time. No, there was no chance for the bread to go bad. It would be devoured before the best by date. We were not supplied with bread as part of our diet.

Eight months into the year, I was told someone wanted to see me at the tents where female combatants lived. With many relatives that passed through our camp, I wondered who it was this time. I got to the tent and greeted whoever I saw first, and announced my presence. Most of them knew me as Fortue's little sister.

"Hey, comrades! Lindi is here, and she says someone told her to come here. Who could that be?" This is the combatant who had promoted me to platoon commander, who was asking her friends.

"Not me," responded some of the combatants. They looked at me, glanced away, and went on with their business. Some were polishing their boots while others were chit-chatting. I was confused. That was strange.

"Sorry, Lindi. Some children are naughty; I am sure they just wanted you to exercise for today," said another one I knew.

"Don't worry about it, just go back and pretend you had a good time with us. Tell them you ate bread," teased another. At that, they all laughed. Bread was not on our diet list, so getting it was considered a special treat.

I was confused by all this, and I wanted to cry due to embarrassment. I turned to leave before anyone could see my tears. Just as I was about to step outside, a hand touched my back and stopped me in my tracks. I turned and came face to face with my sister Fortue (Nhlanhla). I opened my mouth in shock, and no sound came out initially. Since my tears were already on the way, they just ran down my cheeks uncontrollably. I flung my arms around her waist and screamed her name while dancing.

"Nhlanhla!"

"Lee, my little sister!"

We danced around each other for a little while, with tears of joy running down our cheeks. The combat girls were laughing and loving this reunion. They had organized the reunion party and managed to keep my sister's presence a secret. She and other girls had arrived the previous night from Mkushi on their way overseas to further their education. Fortue (as she was known by her nickname) had struggled to spend the night without seeing me, but she had had no choice. We lived under curfew conditions for security reasons. When the initial shock had subsided, we went outside the tent where we could talk without additional ears hearing our conversation. I updated her of the family. She, too, had heard about our sister Orpha's death. We both started crying. We had held the pain inside since we had had no family member to share our grief with. Now the flood gates had been opened. We sobbed and moaned for our sister as if it was the first time we were hearing the news.

Fortue had been brought to VC so she could be vetted to determine if she qualified to further her education.

Like other combatants, she had to be in VC while waiting. Unfortunately for her, she did not qualify for further training. She had repeated her seventh grade after dropping out of her first year in high school. After passing her seventh grade, she had proceeded to do her secondary education at Manama Mission, only to be recruited that very week as she was starting her first year. At sixteen years of age, she had undergone training as a combatant and had risen to the rank of a company commander but could not qualify for a specific career path. We were devastated when we got the news. She was then assigned to guard VC. She was seventeen years at that time.

Because we lived under constant threat of being attacked, one of the threats led us to dig trenches. For that, we had to use the other side of the camp. To counter the threats, security was increased and strengthened. Many combatants had been deployed to guard our camp. Heavy machinery was also brought and deployed around the camp, including anti-air machinery. We felt safer knowing that our camp's security had been tightened.

One day after class, I was sitting in one of the trenches when I saw two male combatants headed in our direction. Although it was not that cold, these two combatants were wearing those thick hats that were worn in colder regions. Judging by their look, we knew they had arrived from training from abroad. My friends and I watched these two guerillas in admiration. As these guerillas got closer, I recognized them, and I flew to meet them. I was sure my eyes were not deceiving me.

"My brother Shepherd!" That was me running to meet my brother.

I could not believe it. My brother Shepherd and Lovett, our cousin and neighbor from Sengezane, had just got back from training from abroad and had been deployed to guard our camp as their first deployment. This was surreal because my sister Fortue was also at the camp as defense personnel. Had it been a time of selfies, this would have made a great profile picture. Females guarded inside the camp while males guarded the outskirts. Information had been passed to my brother that both of us were at the camp. I had last seen him in Selibe-Phikwe in Botswana a year earlier, and I had known his whereabouts too. He had brought me a beautiful watch, my first watch, and I loved it.

Shepherd and Lovett were later moved to train new recruits at Nampundu, a guerilla camp. It was at this camp that Shepherd missed death by a whisker. My brother was later moved to guard many of the party administrative houses that were under constant attack. He survived those many attacks by a whisker.

I met Nothani and cousin Charge at Selibe-Phikwe. After leaving Selibe-Pikwe, Nothani was sent to Nampundu, one of the camps in Zambia. After some vetting, he was sent to JZ camp that housed mostly young boys. It was months later that he was sent to Libya with about seven to eight hundred other boys for further training. He specialized in signals and communications.

My cousin Charge received his training in Nampundu first, then was sent to Angola for further training. Six months later, after training, he was brought to Freedom Camp (FC) in Zambia. He was later deployed along the Zambezi River escarpment at CGT2, where guerillas would cross over from the Zambian side to fight in Zimbabwe. This place was commonly known as *Emagojini* (by the gorges). It was here that they endured constant bombardment by the Rhodesian Army. Several of my cousins, such as Phin, Dan, Enathi, Rueben, and Zathu, were deployed in this area too.

My uncles James and Mpande were fighting on the frontline in Zimbabwe. My uncle James was deployed in the Gweru area while Mpande had been deployed in the Lupane area. They both tell of how they would cross the Zambezi River into Zimbabwe with their arms and how they would fight with the Rhodesian Army. They tell of close calls. Rodgers, our young pastor, had also been deployed in Zimbabwe. He was deployed in the Karoi-Hurungwe area, known as the Northern Front, as regional political commissar. He tells of close calls with the Rhodesian Army. As the world watched, the war intensified, both in and outside Zimbabwe. We would hear of contacts made by the guerillas and would hope for the end of the war.

Meanwhile, like many Zimbabwean families at the time, my family faced significant challenges. After fleeing from the village, my parents went back to Bulawayo, where it had all begun. There, they lived with one of the relatives in his house. They rented one of the rooms and prayed for the war to end. Thando lived with a relative while continuing with her schooling. Emmanuel was also living with another relative. After the death of my sister Orpha, my father, bought a house in the Luveve suburb in Bulawayo.

During that time, the Rhodesian government intensified its national call-up service. A call for national service for White, able-bodied men between the ages of eighteen to thirty-eight had long been instituted. Another call-up for all able-bodied White men between the ages of thirty-eight and fifty years for military service was instituted at the beginning of 1977. Top positions, which were held by White officials, were being left vacant. It is against this backdrop that my brother Emmanuel found himself in a predicament. He was able to find a job at CABS Bank as a bank teller, a position normally held by Whites. As war intensified, however, the Rhodesian government extended its call for national service to include Black men. Emmanuel was forced to quit his job to avoid the call-up.

Having left his position at CABS, my brother Emmanuel interviewed at the National Railways of Zimbabwe (NRZ). Because Whites were leaving the country in droves and some were fighting in the Rhodesian Army, positions for Black people opened. Emmanuel and five other Black males were hired and became the first Black accounting officers at the firm. The looming threat of a call-up caught up with him as White managers were forwarding names of Black men to the government. Many young Black men were forced to leave their jobs and enlist in the army against their will. My big brother was among those who received his call-up letter with his name and a number already written on the letter.

"This is to certify that... National Service Number...is required for National Service intake #...."

He had tried to ignore the letter for three months. But threats of what would happen to him and his family forced him to heed the call. Like many young Black men, they faced a situation they had not anticipated. They were being pitied against their families. The call was divisive in nature.

A tip from one of his mentors was that he should focus on passing his exams with flying colors, so he could spend more time in training than fighting against his kinsmen. He did that, and through training and the selection process, my brother rose to the rank of a lieutenant and was deployed for combat. Although he did even better than the White males in the Rhodesian Army, he would not be promoted to above a lieutenant. He tells many stories of his near-death experience. Since the Rhodesian Army traveled in convoys many times, he faced the risk of being blown away by landmines planted by the guerillas. One time the driver came too close to a trench dug on the road and somehow decided to stop and make a U-turn and have the team proceed on foot. The area was loaded with landmines. They later found out that the road had been set up with a landmine.

My sister Orpha is one unsung hero. Orpha had gone into a coma and had not been able to wake up. She had been taken to Mpilo, where she had failed to wake up. Her funeral had been conducted by guerillas who sang war songs and celebrated her legacy as a ZAPU youth organizer. It was one or more of those guerillas who had traveled back to Zambia for supplies and brought the news of Orpha's death. After hearing the news of this send-off, I was comforted. At least my parents had not been alone. They could have easily buried her alone. At the time of her death, she was getting ready to leave the country to further her studies in the United Kingdom. That never happened.

While in Luveve, one day, two strangers visited my family's home. They asked my parents for fifty supplies of clothing to be brought to them. They claimed to be one group of fighters. My parents asked to be given at least two days so they could collect the supplies. The group left with the understanding that they would return the following day. My parents left that evening and never returned. My sister Thando stayed with her friend. The following day my parents looked for an apartment to rent in the city. They found one and moved.

This was a difficult time for my family and many families in Zimbabwe. My family had been stretched to the limit. Although not a military combatant, my mother was a prayer warrior. She would organize a prayer vigil to pray for the war to end and the safety of her children and that of others. She was a combatant in her own right and an unsung hero.

Chapter 18

The Bombardment

Although we were at school, we lived under frequent threats of bombardments at VC. We were always kept vigilant. Many Selous Scouts had been caught around our camp. One had been caught by the stream where we used to bathe before the construction of the school. Several others had tried to make inroads into the camp. There was a heavily guarded place at VC where these prisoners were kept. The threats were real. We were kept on edge.

As the war intensified in Zimbabwe, the bombing threats became a reality in the camps. We would hear of Rhodesian bombings of guerrilla bases in the Zambezi valley. We would hear of bombings of our neighboring and sister camp, JZ Camp. We would hear of bombings of Nkomo's administrative offices or resident hall. It was a constant threat, left, right, and center! The killing of the ZIPRA commander, Nikita Mangena, was too close to home. We only hoped that the Rhodesian army would consider the fact that ours was a camp for children or a school. We hoped but doubted. For that, we were always prepared for anything.

Our VC had two gates that were manned. We would occasionally see Zambians passing through the camp. Most of the time, they would be accompanied by guerillas to make sure they passed through. One time, two White men drove a tractor through one gate. They had disguised themselves to look like White farmers. Just as they were making their way into the camp, they were stopped and fired with questions. After interrogation, they were found to be members of the Selous Scouts. They carried no iden-tification, but their tractor had been loaded with binoculars and maps. They were taking pictures of the camp. That incident brought so much fear that we could not even sleep for many days. I had nightmares for the longest time.

As evidence of the threats, we lived with members of the Selous Scout who had been captured while trying to penetrate the camp and either cause damage or send report of the camp's map and schedule. An underground pit had been dug to house them. It was creepy. We were afraid of them escaping and causing harm.

UMdala made occasional stops at VC to visit us and keep us hopeful. One day while at parade, and just as he was giving his speech, a bluish helicopter hovered over us and circled around. It looked like it was spying on us. We were quickly told to *"lala phansi,"* take cover, disperse and go into hiding. The ZAPU leader and his convoy quickly exited the camp. We were left dumbfounded and scared. For me, this was the first time facing the enemy at VC. Worse days were yet to come.

Even with the threats, we continued with schooling. As was our custom, my friends and I would sit outside our dorms and wait for the lunch whistle to be blown. Thursdays were our best days. We looked forward to Thursdays, to eating a piece of meat.

We were relaxing outside our dorm one Thursday afternoon on October 19, 1978. Something ominous was taking place around VC that we would soon find out. The Rhodesian Army was launching its first attack on three of the ZAPU camps, Chikumbi, Freedom Camp (FC), and Mkushi. Chikumbi was a refugee camp that housed mostly those who had disabilities, Mkushi was a ZIPRA's training camp for women, while Freedom Camp was ZIPRA's main headquarters and training base for men.

My aunt Moratile (Mora/Abigail) was at Mkushi the day of the bombardment. She tells how she missed death by a whisker. She went to eat early that day and was joking with her friend that she wanted to eat early before being bombed. Little did she know that the bombardment was going to take place that day or week. After eating, she passed through the makeshift toilet, and just as she was relieving herself, a bombardment was made right in front of her. She ducked and miraculously survived that first attack.

Although this was the first bombardment she had witnessed, Abigail's first instinct was to save her company. She ran to her company which was deployed on the eastern side of the camp. The gathering point had swamps, and knowing that the swamps would be impenetrable, she commanded her company to go eastward where there was more cover. She ordered them to keep going until they met Zambian civilians. Her training had been in topography, hence the logical thinking.

Just as she was running and calling her company to keep going eastward, a helicopter hovered over her and made a bombardment. She was covered in blood and dust yet survived again. The Rhodesian Army was releasing tear gases all over the place, and my aunt was finding it difficult to breathe. She collapsed under a thicket, still carrying her AK-47 folded butt. She woke up hours later to the sound of hissing as the Rhodesian Army was dropping napalm all over the place. Napalm was a highly inflammable sticky jelly that adhered to the skin, ignited, and caused severe burns. When combined with water, the burns were unstoppable.

Realizing that she was going to burn alive, she started running for her dear life. A spotter plane had identified her and had started following her. She found a huge tree and took cover under it. Hidden from the spotter plane, she was able to gather strength to run. Her running led her to a stream that was covered with reeds. Since she was not a swimmer, she stood there for a while, wondering what to do next. Most Zambian streams are muddy, not sandy, so she was unsure how deep the water was. She threw her gun over the stream, gathered some courage, held on to some reeds, and crossed over. She followed some footprints and was able to get to the nearest Zambian police camp. That is how she survived the brutal attack by the Rhodesian Army. She was later able to help those who were injured. Her company survived this brutality, but many lives were lost that day.

While my friends and I were relaxing outside our dorm, we heard warning shots being fired with urgency, indicating there was no time to waste. Fortunately for my friends and me, since we were already outside, we immediately threw ourselves onto the ground to take cover. At the sound of the next gunshot, we knew what we had to do. Our dorm was at the edge of the fence, so we were fortunate that the fleeing direction favored us. We ran out of the camp, and we knew where to run. To the stream, we took off.

Just as we were running out of camp, a distant sound of bombardment was heard. It was a rumble in the jungle. Since Freedom Camp was in the same Lusaka area as VC, we could hear the bombings. I knew that we were in big trouble, and I immediately got into survival mode. As shots were being fired everywhere, panic and pandemonium ensued as people were coming out of their dorms, taking cover, and/or running to the gathering point. Just as we were running to the designated point, two jet fighters suddenly appeared from nowhere, flying low and at an alarming speed. I threw myself on the ground and crawled to the nearest bush to take cover. The jet fighters circled around the camp. And just as they had appeared, they suddenly disappeared. This time, gunshots were being fired everywhere.

I got up as soon as the jets had disappeared and ran as fast as I could toward the stream. I was crouching as I was running. I would throw myself on the ground if there was not enough cover and crawl to the nearest bush. I did this until I got to the stream. Those who had been caught up in the middle of the camp had to run all the way to the stream. The stream provided some cover as there were bushes there. I crossed the stream and stayed under the bushes with everyone, and we waited for our death sentence or survival.

This area had been abandoned as toilets once the dorms had been built. Now it was home to human waste and fire ants. Talk about being bombarded in all directions! The fire ants were out with vengeance. The smell of human waste was sickening. We were trapped! We had used that part of the bush as toilets; now, we were hiding from the Rhodesian Army at that same place. My desire at this point was to throw myself into the water to flee from the fire ants, but that would have been suicidal since it was not part of the order. We spent the whole day in hiding.

Closely guarding us was none other than my sister Fortue as one of the combatants. In her combat uniform and with a gun in hand, she stood ready to defend her territory. *If we were to die that day,* I thought to myself, *we would have died together. Would my family ever know that she would have died defending children? Would they know that her little sister was there with her?* Fear gripped me.

We had faced constant threats, but never of this magnitude.

Towards the evening, we cautiously approached the camp in small groups to get food and blankets. There was no time for second helpings of meat this time; this was a somber day. We spent days in the bush, not knowing if or when the Rhodesian army would strike again. We would occasionally go into the camp for food, that is, if it was available. With or without blankets, cold nights would wreak havoc on us. Most of us lost track of time during this period. Once it was determined that the threat was over, we went back to camp, and life resumed as usual. No bombings had been made on our camp at that time. Another thing that always blows my mind is that none of us ever got bitten by snakes while living in the bush. We were all accounted for and in one piece.

News traveled fast at VC. We were usually kept abreast of any security breaches. Thousands of people had died in those camps. Many of my relatives had passed through those camps and were either out of the country or guarding VC. This included my sister. I could not call this luck; it was God's grace. My sister had just left Mkushi a month earlier. I could not even imagine what was going through her mind at this time. Most of Manama students were at the Mkushi Camp. Fortue had been brought to VC so she could travel out of the country to further her education, just like all others. While she was being vetted to determine her eligibility, she had been assigned as one of the military guards at VC.

We heard that the raid by the Rhodesian Army had been supported by helicopter gunships, paratroopers, and ground ambush. We also heard that the Rhodesian army had used napalm, a highly inflammable sticky jelly. The weapon adhered to the skin, ignited, and caused severe burns. When combined with water, the burns were unstoppable. Because of this information, we were moved away from the river to a different location outside the camp.

Our VC housed a large armory. With the bombings of Mkushi and Freedom Camp, the armory was quickly moved to a different location. Intelligence had picked it that its presence at the camp made it a target and posed risks for VC. The Rhodesian Army had known about the armory and was now targeting it. The bombings had caught ZAPU and ZIPRA unawares. They started beefing up the camp with bazookas and anti-aircraft machines, known as ZAG-U.

The bombing of Mkushi and FC also taught us about napalm. This highly inflammable sticky jelly was used by the Rhodesian Army to inflict burns on ZAPU combatants. As a result of that, we were made to dig defense pits. Defense pits were dug downwards first and were to be almost as deep as the individual's height. They would then be dug horizontally to fit the length of one's body. It was a scary endeavor at first, as we felt like we were digging our own graves. We eventually got used to staying in the defense pits. I dug my pit with the help of my soldier sister. She still felt responsible for me even though I was a teenager then, a thirteen-year-old.

Defense pits would either be one's grave or saving grace. My brother Shepherd tells of his experience in Nampundu, where he was a trainer for new recruits. One day he and Lovett were walking towards the kitchen for lunch, as others were already gathered there. Just as he looked up, the sky had suddenly darkened. The Rhodesian jet fighters suddenly appeared from nowhere and darkened the sky. Bombs and napalm were being dropped from the sky. Huge explosions were heard, and smoke was seen from the direction of the kitchen where most combatants were gathering for lunch. Helicopters were hovering above the camp and firing like crazy. My brother and Lovett ran toward the kitchen area, firing back at the Rhodesian helicopters, but it was impenetrable. He took cover in the defense pit until the attack was over. Many lives were lost that day. Their survival had been incredible.

Besides protecting us from napalm, pits also protected us from flying debris or shrapnel. We had learned that our water tank was a double-edged sword. While it stored water for the camp, it was also a target for the Rhodesian Army. By bombing it, it would splinter and send shrapnel to kill those around. Defense pits were dug to protect us from our water tank and napalm. An anti-aircraft system was strategically lodged outside the camp, in view of the tank and in anticipation of the direction of the would-be enemy jet fighters. We felt safer in defense pits than in the dorms. We spent most of the day hanging out and doing our homework at our defense pits. We would go to our dorms for the night.

For me, defense pits provided privacy as well as a place of entertainment that we otherwise did not have. It was in those pits that I would remember my teachers, Mrs. Mkandla, who I called Mrs. Nkandla, and Mrs. Siwawa. I would remember my preschool days and sing the rhymes and act them out to my friends. Most of them had grown up in rural Gwanda; they had not attended preschool and had never lived in the city. So, my acting provided entertainment as I would talk about my childhood stunts. This provided some temporal relief from anxiety. I would talk about my first-grade teacher, Mrs. Siwawa, and how she had helped me master the isiNdebele orthography by second-grade level. During the school holiday, some of us would write short novels in isiNdebele and present them as free literature and entertainment to others.

It was in my defense pit that I would dream of a free Zimbabwe. We had been taught about inequalities and the treatment of Black people. Thus, I would dream of a land of opportunities. I would imagine myself being educated, having a beautiful home, and a family of my own.

I would imagine Ross Camp, our infamous toilet, hunting locusts, roasting them, and my bike ride with my brave sister Thando. I would wonder if she missed me the way I did. I would think of my brother Emmanuel and his never-ending story of Georgy Mganu. I would retell the story to my friends, teach them the song *"Sasihamba eGoli"* that my brother had composed. We would dance while singing it. We would be entertained.

I knew about call-up and that he had been enlisted in the Rhodesian Army as was required by the then government. I would worry about my brother fighting against his brother, as I knew where he stood politically. I would think of my sister Orpha, and the loss would be too deep. I would sob. I would feel sorry for myself. I would feel sorry for my mother. How could a mother lose her child? How could she lose all her children? I would think of my hero, my father, an honorable and selfless man. I would think of his brood, all torn apart. The thought of his chuckle would bring back a smile.

My mother had taught me how to pray. She had told me that God heard even the shortest prayer, a phrase, a word if it came from the heart. As it became apparent that the war was not going to end in a few days, I did not know how else to pray for the war to end. I lost words. I was at a point where I could not pray. I hoped that God would hear as my mother had said. I would find myself uttering phrases like, "Oh, God," "Lord, help," "My God," or "Please, Lord." Many times, it would be just calling on the name "Jesus" or "God" and asking for protection. It was during these times in my self-defense pit that I would wonder if God was listening to my prayer. I would hope He was listening, as my mother had told me.

It was in these defense pits that I would dream of a peaceful life away from guns, fear, anxiety, and hopelessness. I would dream of a peaceful life with the man of my dreams. I would create a perfect character in my mind, a loving man, a man who would understand the trauma exerted on me, a man who would seek my happiness, a man who would be my pillar. I dreamed to keep myself sane.

I would look at the sun, the stars, and the moon and wonder if my family was seeing the same galaxy I was seeing. I did not know my geography in relation to the camp, so I could not tell where Zimbabwe was.

It was in my defense pit where I would sob. As the endless war and the perpetual threat of being bombed continued to loom, it took toll on my psychological well-being, and I would be in a state of hopelessness. Although we were constantly updated to raise our morale, many times, I sank into hopelessness. During the holidays, I would lose track of time. My friends and I would not even know the days and dates. We just existed through the long and dreary days. Dreaming kept me going. A flashback of commemorative events would revive my state of mind. I would draw my strength from reliving my otherwise happy childhood, my journey, and the people that would have positively impacted me. I would draw on these people and events to revive my psyche in my dire most time of need. I would be revived from my state of hopelessness and would hope again.

After school, we would go to our defense pits and wait for our meal call. One day we were busy playing close to our defense pits, when a warning shot was given. We scurried and got into our pits. In the blink of an eye, we saw four jet fighters approaching from the direction of our water tank. They were coming from the same direction that intelligence had indicated. As they approached, they were met with a missile from our anti-aircraft system. We heard the heavy sound of contact between the airplane and the missile. We popped our small heads out of our defense pits and watched this wonder. We witnessed the tail of one plane on fire. The planes never managed to make the bombing. They met their fate before we could meet ours.

Instead of waiting for a signal to indicate it was safe to come out, we peeped our small heads out of our defense pits and clapped. Some of us took a further step and got out and skipped and danced in celebration. We chanted.

"Wayitshay' ubhud' uMgco! Wayitshay' ubhud' uMgco!" (Our brother Mgco hit it!)

We erupted in celebration as we saw that plane in flames. A gunshot over our heads warned us that it was too early to celebrate. We got back into our defense pits but kept our heads peeping in case there was another fighter jet to meet the same fate as the one we had just witnessed. The guerillas who manned the machine were affectionately known as *"obhudi,"* our brothers. Mgcozo rarely left his seat. We would see him occasionally passing by our defense pits on his way to get food from the kitchen. We would wave at him with so much adoration. He was on the seat that day, manning the anti-aircraft machine as always, hence our praise of him.

As was always the case, one Thursday afternoon, either in February or early March 1979, my friends and I were sitting outside our dorm one day, talking and laughing. It was a day we all looked forward to because we would have meat served. That day I was suffering from tonsillitis, my mother's curse. While waiting for the dining signal, I lay down and supported my head on Ally's thigh. I was feeling weak due to tonsillitis. We suddenly heard a gunshot warning and knew we were in trouble. Our dorm was at the end toward the fence. This position had worked for us the first time we had to flee from the camp to the stream. This time the signal indicated that we had to go out through the gate. Unfortunately, that day our fleeing route was all the way down through several dorms and out the gate.

We started running all the way past the dorms to the

gate. As we were three-quarters of the way in the camp, about a quarter away from the gate, my body failed me. I was weak. I was now between the water tank (which was considered a target) and the gate. I started walking instead of running. The area was plain; there were no trees or shrubs. I was a moving target. All the basic training I had had could not work.

This time reminded me of the time when I was crossing the Shashi River into Botswana just a year or so earlier. I had been in the same predicament. Tonsillitis! They seemed to attack me at the wrong time. I found myself giving up on life for the second time. I faced death, and I gave up. Running and tonsillitis do not seem to coordinate, I have concluded.

Gunshots were flying over me as a sign that I was becoming a target and putting everyone at risk. This area had no trees; it was just bare. Based on the sound of the gunshots, I knew I still had a chance to run out of the camp if only my legs could carry me just a little further. If you have ever had a dream where you are running, but you are failing to make strides, you will understand what was happening to me. It's like you are floating in the air.

As I got closer to the security manning the anti-aircraft

machine, I could hear an LMG or an RKP rapidly firing over my head. I could smell the gun smoke and see fireballs before and above me. At that time, they had not yet started the anti-aircraft machine. The jets were expected to come from behind me, anytime, by way of the water tank. Intelligence had picked that our water tank was the target because it would provide shrapnel that would target us as we would be running. There were no trees to hide. I could see no more than four bodies in the camp at that time. Ally was one of them and two or so elderly women. Ally was an athlete; she could outrun most people, but this time she kept holding back so I could reach her. She started begging me,

"Run, Lindi, please! Run! Run! Run! How can you be outrun by elderly women?"

"I cannot do it, Ally; please run and be safe. It's okay to leave me behind. Run! Run!"

"No, Lindi, no, Lindi, I cannot leave you behind. Please run. You can do it! Run! Run!"

We were exchanging words of encouragement to each other. I knew I could not run any further; I was weak. I did not want to fall and be unable to raise my body, so I decided to face death. Ally was going crazy at this moment, running and turning to plead with me. She was talking to herself at that moment. I had already given up. And yes, she was right. I could see two elderly women, one with a long skirt and the other with a long dress flying toward the gate. "Whatever is going to happen to me, at this point, let it be. I am going to walk through the last distance." I said to myself and started walking.

"Nkulunkulu wami!" (My God). I started calling on the name of God. This name of God means "the Big One" or "the Great One." I could almost hear myself uttering that name repeatedly as I was walking.

Ally was still running and turning to check if I was following her. She had held my hand all the way from the dormitory, and once I realized that I was slowing her, I let go of her hand. She had to follow the command, too, as the female combatant was calling on us to run. She made it out of the camp and took cover by the bushes. At that point, the only body I could see in the camp was mine and that of one of the female combatants that guarded us. She was squatting and waiting for me by the gate, encouraging me to run. I could not hear what she was saying due to the noise made by the gunshots above me but could see her hands moving back and forth, encouraging me to keep moving.

313

Suddenly, I felt strengthened. I started running again, this time with speed and renewed strength. I somehow knew I had no time left. I ran straight out of the gate and behind the ant hill that housed the anti-aircraft and was directed to move to the side. I crawled to look for a hiding spot close to where I thought I would find Ally. As soon as I could find a bush and take cover, the anti-aircraft machine was let loose in time to unleash its missiles. Two Rhodesian jet fighters, which were now flying over our water tank, were met with the missiles, and their fate was determined. This was the same direction that the intelligence team had picked. It was the loudest noise ever. The jets had been hit before dumping their bombs. All I could see was black smoke. We heard they had just bombed our sister camp, JZ Camp, which was a school for boys. Memory of those jets has lingered in my mind for as long as I can remember.

When it was considered safe, Ally and I went in search of others. We were all accounted for. We were led to an area further from our VC. Later in the evening, we trickled in from the bush to get some food. A few of our kitchen staff had snuck in to prepare and serve the food. Most of the food had already been prepared before the warning shots were fired. We got our food, ate while standing, washed the dishes, and went back to the bush.

We stayed for some days in the bush, not knowing if the Rhodesian Army would strike again. With the hitting of the jets, it could not be determined when retaliation could take place. It was necessary to be cautious in case the enemy was planning yet another attack. For that, we stayed in the bush a few more days. Each day dragged its feet and felt longer than normal. It became difficult to keep up with time. We just existed. There are days when it rained. This was a challenge for the kitchen staff. On those days, we would eat very late. Our *isitshwala* (pap/sadza/nsima/ugali) would be soaking wet, and the broth would be tasteless. We stayed in the bush for days until it was determined that we were safe. For me, this day has been playing in my mind for as long as I can remember.

As the war intensified, we would hear gunshots daily. Spotter planes, jets, and helicopters hovering above our camp became the order of the day. We got so exhausted as each day dragged along the perpetual threats of being bombarded. As our sister camp, JZ, continued being bombarded, we became hopeless. We would be uplifted when anti-aircraft missiles were fired, and the aircrafts would be hit or disappear for that time.

Young as most of us were, we got used to the sounds of guns such that they became part of us. I remember one time, we had stayed a couple of days without hearing gunshots, we started missing the sounds. We begged our guards to just shoot in the air. Just once. They would comply, and we would be so happy. Thinking about it now as an adult, I wonder what psychologists would say about us.

Chapter 19

The Repatriation

While the war was raging on, ceasefire talks were also underway and were promising a better ending. On the twenty-first of December 1979, a ceasefire agreement was brokered through the Lancaster House Agreement. It was during this period that combatants were being removed from our camp and taken to their camps in preparation for repatriation.

During the cease-fire, we started hearing details about our families' whereabouts. It was confirmed that mine was in Bulawayo. I still could not identify who was giving me the updates. But somehow, I was informed.

Guerillas were repatriated first and sent to assembly points. After independence, they were integrated into one army, the Zimbabwe National Army. My brother Emmanuel, as a lieutenant, was selected to train as one of the integration officers to integrate the fighting forces into one army, the Zimbabwe National Army. He underwent training and was sent to Imbizo Barracks, where he and other officers worked at integrating different fighting forces into a national army.

My sister Fortue got sick with tonsillitis. They were so bad to the extent of causing the lower part of her face to swell. She could not eat. I asked why she had not been sent to Lusaka for treatment. Her response was that she could not go for treatment because she was required to be at her camp in Solwezi in preparation for the repatriation. I was furious but could not challenge anyone at that time. There is a lot I did not know.

She hoped to receive treatment at the camp. Judging by the fact that the camp was new, I doubted if that was a good idea. Young as I was, I knew this was a bad idea. I was saddened by the whole situation; I considered it as negligence. I was furious but could not do anything.

And for sure, a day later, before her departure, she surrendered everything she had borrowed from me, including my watch that my brother Shepherd had given me. I was saddened by this gesture. I went to bid her farewell later that afternoon. We talked for a while before she got into the truck.

"MaLi, I don't think I will see you again. I am going home," my sister Fortue said as the other female combatants were getting into the truck.

Ignoring what I thought this statement could mean, I commented,

"At least you will see our family before long."

"Bye, my little sister. Do not worry about me. I will be fine soon. I love you."

We embraced, and I sobbed on her shoulder. After a moment, we let go. I was expecting her to get into the truck, but she did not. She stood still. My sister Fortue was the only one among the female combatants who was still outside the truck. I moved away from her, but she inched closer. We hugged again. We let go, but she still would not budge. We looked at each other with tears running down our cheeks. One of their commanders, tired of waiting and watching this act, came and asked her to get into the truck. If I had my way, I would not have let her go. My heart just broke, and I could not control myself. I sobbed right there before the truck could leave. It took me a while to recover, wipe my face, and head to the dormitory.

A week later, I was sitting in my dorm when Sithabile came and told me that we were being called by Country girl. I was concerned because she normally called me to deliver bad news. I did not want to go and therefore asked

Sithabile to tell her I would come later. After about half an hour, I saw Sithabile coming to my dorm again. She asked me to come with her, and I still refused. She begged until I gave in and went with her. We got in Aunt Country girl's dorm and sat on the floor. We greeted each other, and after the greetings, she spoke in SeSotho and said,

"Ahh, cousin has passed on."

Sithabile started crying, and I just looked down to show respect for the departed. I did not know which cousin had passed on since she had not said the name. After a while, I excused myself, so I could go back to the dorm. Sithabile excused herself too and followed me. After a few yards, I turned and asked Sithabile about who had died.

"Ahh, you do not know?" Sithabile asked in surprise.

"Of course not. How could I have known when Country girl reported in SeSotho. We have a thousand cousins; how could I have known which one? She said, *'bokhazini balobile'* (our cousin passed away). How could I have known which one?"

I was now yelling at Sithabile as if she was the one who had reported a dead cousin. I could feel all the anger, fear, and agitation of the war pilling up, and Sithabile seemed to have been the nearest punchbag at that time.

"Okay. Let us go back so she can tell you."

At that, she saw the other side of me that she had never seen. I was normally a mellow child, but that day, I was furious and took it all upon Sithabile. I did not raise my voice, which was typical of me. I lowered my voice instead and emphatically responded,

"No! I am not going back in there again! She is tasked with telling me bad news; as an adult, I expect her to be able to do so. I am not going back there. I do not even want to know who died at this time. I am tired of hearing about people dying. Who will be left? We are going to go home and find who? Who? You tell me. No, you go back alone and tell her I still do not know who died, and I do not want to know!"

To say Sithabile was stunned is an understatement. She was horrified and looked at me as if she was seeing a ghost. She looked like she was wondering how she could handle me at that time. She stood motionless while I turned and walked toward my dorm.

"Wait, Lili, my girl." That is what she called me.

I stopped and waited for her. She caught up with me.

"Please, promise that we will both go back to cousin after I tell you," she begged.

"Nope, I said I am not going back there again. Are you going to tell me or what? And please do not say it's my sister who died."

At that, Sithabile's mouth went agape. She froze. I had not expected that response. I now feared the worst.

"It is Fortue," the words came out from Sithabile's mouth with difficulty.

"Ahh!" that is all that could come out of my mouth.

I turned and uttered no other word and headed straight to my dormitory. She followed me, but I was not talking to her. Different emotions were running through my body and mind. My sister was gone. It was like a dream. I floated to my dorm and went straight into my bed, and covered myself in my blanket. I was grieving alone for the second time. I sobbed uncontrollably. Life was unfair. Our country was just about to become independent. This was December 1979, and the peace talks were promising an independent Zimbabwe in four months and a reunion with our families. Why couldn't someone send her to the hospital? Why? Why? So close, Fortue, so close. I cried with no one to console me.

The days ahead were very difficult for me. There was nothing that my friends could do in situations like these. None of us had learned the art of comforting others. We could not even talk it out. We did not know how. We just continued living and not knowing what to say and do. We knew we had each other. Just their presence was enough. But the pain, no one could carry that for you. It was like dying. People may be there to support you, but death is experienced by an individual. That is how I felt. My pain could not be shared. Had I been with my family, or at least one member, we would have shared the pain. We would have grieved together.

Years later, I met one former combatant who told me that Fortue had been laid with a full twenty-one-gun salute. That brought joy to my heart. She said Fortue had died of typhoid. How? I wondered because no one else at Solwezi Camp beside her had been diagnosed with typhoid. She had been sent to the hospital at Solwezi, and they had diagnosed her with typhoid. Hmm. She had died less than a week after leaving VC. She is one of those warriors whose graves lie away from their homeland. She was buried next to another girl who had been accidentally shot. The only two graves in that camp. Her grave was never marked, and I wonder who knows where it is. My sister, you will always be remembered with love. I could only hope that one day I could go and find where your bones were laid to bring closure to my heart. Meeting you in heaven, and hearing your beautiful voice, would be the utmost blessing for me.

It was on the eighteenth of April 1980 that Zimbabwe became independent. We could not contain the joy of being free at last and being reunited with our families. It was surreal. The repatriation exercise for school-aged children at VC did not take place until towards the end of September 1980, several months into Zimbabwe's independence. Since we were no longer living under threats of bombardment, we were able to patiently wait our turn. We ate well, slept well, and enjoyed our schooling. We were kept abreast of the repatriation exercise and the challenges. We were kept entertained by musical groups that visited us, watching movies, and having disco nights; it was life again. We did all this at our parade, which no longer harbored lice. Celebratory songs of freedom would be heard all over the camp. We would sing, harmonize, and dance to our hearts' desires. No fear. No anxiety. We were free!

"*Yithi laba, esasingekho* (Here we are, those of us who were away)

Yithi laba, bon'okijana (Here we are, the kids)

Esasithiwa, s'ngamagandanga (Who were called freedom fighters)

Esasithiwa, sngamatororo" (Who were called terrorists)

Sikhokhele Nkomo, singene eZimbabwe." (Lead us, Joshua Nkomo, into Zimbabwe[2])

The song no longer brought sorrow as before. We no longer had to spend nights in the bush. We slept peacefully in our dormitories. "Sijabule Namhlanje" by the LMG choir was one of our favorite songs.

It was also during this time that we were able to receive letters from our families. I received one from my sister Thando. She was doing her Advanced Level (Twelfth Grade) at the time. She sent me pictures of our family, including that of my brother Shepherd who had joined them. It was surreal. I looked forward to finally being reunited with them.

During the August-September school holiday, our teachers left so they could be reunited with their families before they could meet us at our designated school to finish the year. Two choirs that had been formed by Mr. Give Nare and Mr. Mtshibete had departed before independence.

2 H. Sibanda and the LMG Choir "Sijabule Namhlanje." YouTube, October 31, 2020.

It was at the end of September 1980, exactly three years after leaving Zimbabwe, that we were finally repatriated. The first repatriation batch of children included children who were doing their secondary education at the time. I was fifteen years old by then and doing Form One (equivalent to Eighth Grade in the US).

The day of our repatriation marked one of the best days of my life. Once our repatriation date was announced, we sang songs of joy wherever we were. One such song was in praise of the United Buses of Zambia (UBZ) since they were tasked with ferrying us to the train station. We would sing and dance and laugh.

iUBZ uma ibuya ngiyareya (When the UBZ comes, I will go)

iUBZ uma ibuya ngiyakhwela (When the UBZ comes, I will leave)

iUBZ! UBZ! UBZ! UBZ!

The United Buses of Zambia (UBZ) were sent to pick us up from VC and drop us at the railway station in Lusaka. We got there early in the morning and were given food to eat. We were going home. We got on the train and headed south to our homeland. It was surreal. For most of us, this was the first time being on a train. We traveled the whole day and the whole night. My friends and I made sure we were awake to witness the train crossing the Zambezi River into Zimbabwe.

Early in the morning of the following day, we crossed the border. There was the magnificent Zambezi River and her spectacular Victoria Falls. We could hear the thundering as the water fell deep into the Zambezi gorge. With our heads peeping out of the windows and arms stretched out, the feeling of mist on our bodies soothed our traumatized souls. We were home. Having spent three years locked up in one place, living a hopeless life, seeing only trees, grass, and our camp buildings, I felt like this breathtaking view was like a soothing ointment that runs down from one's head to the soles of one's feet. The excitement was off the charts!

We finally arrived in Bulawayo later that afternoon, on the second day. We were picked up by buses which took us to Luveve suburb where tents were prepared for our arrival.

In our tents, before being reunited with our families, my friends and I had practiced how we were going to react to our family. We were going to act "cool" by not jumping and throwing ourselves at them. We practiced walking with a limp, shifting one's body to the side. That was a "cool" greeting from someone who had fought the war, we thought. We were not going to cry. We were going to look super cool. We agreed.

During the visitors' time, we would sit in our tents and wait to hear if our names were called through a megaphone. I heard mine and went out of my tent to meet my first guest. I did not know who it was. Standing tall to welcome his daughter was my father, my hero! I will never forget that first reunion. His smile, his chuckle, radiated and illuminated my heart. That smile had kept me going for three years. He had not aged. I was grown. I ran and threw myself on him, forgetting completely about what we had practiced. I could have knocked him down had it not been for the fact that he was still as strong as a horse. We embraced for a while, and we started laughing. Unbelievable! We started laughing. He would laugh and hug me, laugh, and hug me. For quite some time, we carried out this demonstration of love. It was interesting to watch. I could tell by the laughter that it caused to the onlookers.

Having asked for permission to take me home for the afternoon, hand in hand, we made our way out of the camp. He took me home to show me my new home and brought me back at the scheduled time. We were to stay at the camp until the end of the week before being carried off to our school to complete the year.

I saw my sister Thando later that day. My sister's stories had kept me hoping when I had lost hope. I would sit in my defense pit and think about my sister, the many stories we had shared, and the laughter. I would tell Aziko story to my friends, and we would roll out with laughter. Everyone knew I had a sister named Thando. They had to know. Many times, I would sink into hopelessness, but thinking about my sister would give me hope. I would tell stories about her to my friends, and we would laugh and forget about the endless war. We would encourage one another and plan what we would do the day we saw them. That day finally came. When I saw my sister, I flew and flung my arms across her waist. We jumped up and down in excitement. I am normally less talkative than my sister, but that day, I was telling her everything I could tell her in half an hour. We were chatting as if continuing a story that had been left incomplete. It was a great reunion.

I saw my brother Emmanuel next. He still held the same chuckle and mischievous smile. As my big brother, he was also my best friend. I had told his never-ending stories of Georgy Mganu to my friends many times to keep us entertained. We would dance around our defense pits to many songs, including the one that he had composed after I had told him about my sisters passing gas while we were sleeping. The singing had kept us going when we would have fallen apart. Our reunion was capped with laughter and joy.

The last person I saw was my mother. I saw her last because she was teaching out of the city at the time and had to wait until the end of the week to come to the city. When my name was called, I did not know who the visitor was. I was expecting to see my mother the following day on Saturday. I went to the reception area in response to the call. My mother saw me first and waved at me. If I was a bird, I would have easily taken off and flown to her side. I ran in her direction, pushing and shoving whoever was on my way. With arms wide open, I flung myself over her and tightly gripped her waist.

"Mama! Mama!"

"MaLi!"

Here was an unsung hero. She had birthed many war-riors. She had not fought with arms or weapons; she had fought on her knees. She would organize prayer groups locally, nationally, and internationally. She had knelt, humbled herself, and prayed for her family and for the country. She had lost children during the time but had continued to believe in the God whose thoughts and ways are higher than ours. She believed in the God whose hand is not shortened to save and whose ear is not heavy to listen. She believed in the Creator of the universe, who neither faints nor is weary, whose understanding is unsearchable, who gives power to the weak, and strength to those who have no might. She was a prayer warrior. My family and many others were the beneficiaries of those prayers and tears. She represented many people who fought by faith.

"My child, it is you. You are grown. You are the Guarded One, as your name says. *Ulindwe yiNkosi* (You are one guarded by the Lord). God looked after you, and He will continue looking after you."

I could imagine mother and daughter erupting with a song.

"This is the day, this is the day, that the Lord has made.

We will rejoice, we will rejoice and be glad in it..."

For my mother and me, the Book of Psalm 118 verse 24 came alive that day. I held on to my dear mother as if afraid someone would pull me away. Years of pain and suffering, fear, anxiety, loss, and hopelessness, finally found a shoulder to cry on. I sobbed. We did not speak for a long time; we just embraced and cried. Our hearts spoke. Mother and daughter were finally reunited.

Chapter 20

The Integration

After a week of meeting with our families, those of us who were in high school were sent to Wanezi Mission to finish the school year. Wanezi Mission had been closed during the war, and we were the first group to reopen it after independence. My mother was a constant visitor to my school. She could not spend a week without seeing me. At the end of the year, my parents came to pick me up and sought a transfer letter from Principal Matjaka. This time, I bid farewell to my friends. I knew I was not going to be with them the following year. There was no way my mother would let me out of her sight again.

My friends and I faced many challenges as we integrated into society. As my parents sought placement for my Form Two, they found that there was an influx of students in secondary schools that year in Bulawayo and elsewhere. Independence had made it possible to open schools that had been closed. Mandatory education had led to higher enrollment. My parents sought a good school for me but could not find what they had wanted. At the very last minute, I got enrolled at Njube Secondary School through my sister's contact, Sphumu Mgodla, who was a teacher and our neighbor. It was there where I completed my secondary education.

Before independence, Njube High School had been ranked as an F2 school, which was a lower rank compared to other schools. It went from Grade Eight to Grade Eleven. The curriculum focused on practical and technical subjects. After independence, four-year schooling was introduced to the F2 schools. I joined Njube after independence. My classmates had done Grade Eight and then had to go back and start Form One. I found them in Form Two, having completed two years of secondary education while I had only completed one year. I found myself behind in many of the subjects, especially practical ones like Food and Nutrition and Fashion and Fabrics.

I was introduced to practical subjects for the first time while my classmates were doing their third year of practical subjects. I was far behind. My Fashion and Fabrics teacher hated me with passion because I would ask her to help me thread the sewing machine, show me how to cut the materials, and how to make the different types of stitches. That kept her up from her chair and away from doing whatever she would have planned to do while her students were sewing. I would ask so many questions, and she would be annoyed. I failed the class that whole year.

For the Food and Nutrition class, I did not know how to cook anything! I did not even know how to turn the stove on. Language used to describe recipes, equipment and utensils was just confusing to me. Fortunately, all Form Twos (Grade Nine) were assessed at the end of the first term, and I qualified for what was known as the "A" stream, those who could be ready to write their Ordinary Level after two years from that time. With a different teacher for my Fashion and Fabrics class the following year, my life changed. She showed interest in me and believed in me. I found myself doing even better than my classmates in that subject. Our class was required to drop the Food and Nutrition class.

As we integrated into society, we were met with animosity. Some people continued referring to us as refugees. This was puzzling and upsetting as we were now living in our own country. This behavior, as I saw it, for some was due to lack of knowledge of what the word meant. Some families had no concept of being a refugee, as they did not have family members leave the country and assume refugee statuses. For others, however, it was meant to cause pain and ridicule. Such an address was meant to make one feel better about not having participated in the struggle in any manner.

I remember one day at Njube High School, I saw this boy who used to walk around the school and seemed to know everything and everyone. He approached this girl who had been with me at VC and asked her where she had been the previous year. The girl had responded innocently by telling the truth. This boy turned to make sure everyone around would hear what this girl had said. He started laughing and pointing at that girl.

"Ha! Ha! Ha! Ha! She is a refugee! She is a refugee!" he mocked.

I was stunned and saddened by this behavior. I got to know this boy and forgave him, too, since we were later put in the same class. I never revealed my status to him or anyone in my class or school for fear of ridicule. It was only my cousin Nothando and best friend Colletor who knew my status. My cousin Nothando, being close to me in age, contributed to my healing. She was the curious one who would ask even the silliest questions. I would satisfy her curiosity by telling her even the most difficult stories, and we would also find something to laugh about. In her eyes, I was a hero, an overcomer, and her role model. I had to confide with Colletor since she had to understand the reason for my struggle in practical subjects. I was comfortable sharing that information with her.

My friend Colletor and me.

Some people try to make themselves feel better by demeaning others. For a while, we lived with being labeled as refugees in a country whose liberation we had significantly contributed to. Our presence in refugee camps as children brought to light the plight of Black Zimbabweans. Resistance by the Rhodesian minority government led to international pressure to heed the cry for majority rule.

Psychologically, we were impacted. Many of my friends and I felt like we were losers due to the ridicule. To avoid being a subject of ridicule, we distanced and hid our identity. We never told our story. We were a scenario that never existed. While in Zambia, we would receive donated clothing from many nations globally. Because we could be easily identified by our clothes, I had to get rid of them, so I could fit in. Now that I am older and wiser, I wish I had kept at least one for memories.

Many of my peers found themselves as social misfits. We had to learn the culture, the food, and the colloquial language.

For three years, we had lived without having contact with the opposite sex. The only males we saw were the adults who took care of us and a few young boys who were too young to be at our sister camp for boys, JZ Camp. For some, this was problematic because the moment they were repatriated, they had unplanned pregnancies. This could have been due to many factors, such as lack of knowledge on how to navigate the sexual scene appropriately or abuses that they may have fallen victim to. Due to the un-planned pregnancies, some were unable to complete their secondary education and better themselves.

Although we were all afforded the opportunity to continue with our schooling, having a support system that values education is important. My family was my support system, and their value of education helped guide me. Others came home and did not find a support system and thus, were unable to integrate effectively and complete their schooling.

As I interviewed my friends for this book, I was surprised at the many details they had forgotten. Off-course, the fact that this is written many years later, forty-two years to be precise, would largely explain the information decay. The brain deals with trauma in various ways. Information decay happens when information is not revisited and used, or if information is associated with painful events, the brain suppresses it as a way of healing. That is how I assessed my friend's forgetfulness. One of them even forgot what we used to eat. The only food she could remember was the notorious wild beans, *umtshatshatsha*. Of course, no one seems to have forgotten this delicacy, mostly because it was a novel food which we associated with goats. Since I was able to talk about my experiences with my friends and family, I found that I still remembered as much as possible. The fact that I have always had a good memory goes in my favor, too.

For me, healing came about as I maintained my friendships. We would visit one another and talk about our experiences. We would laugh even at those situations that would have been difficult at the time. I found that talking and laughing about these experiences helped me get through the trauma. I could not tell my family everything that I had experienced, as it caused so much pain. My mother would not even want me to tell her anything. Talking to my friends helped me go through the healing process. Not all former refugees were able to do so.

As I matured, I would find any opportunity to tell part of my story to those close to me. Others found it difficult to tell their story even as adults, to the extent that they would not even divulge their participation to their significant other and family. As a result, their story is unknown.

Due to the perpetual flashback of events during my time as a refugee, I have written my story over and over in my mind, hoping that one day I would write it down on paper and share it with the world. The process has been healing for me.

Chapter 21

The Reflection

As the world becomes a global village and wars are fought, refugee children will continue to be a concern. Childhood refugee trauma has been found to affect mental, physical, and/or emotional health of a child even long after the events have occurred. According to Dye (2018), early childhood trauma can impact human development and cause significant changes in brain function. Due to childhood refugee trauma, some children may have difficulty grasping information and understanding concepts. From this perspective, I wonder at the percentage of VC (or even JZ) children who made it into colleges and universities. A study to examine this phenomenon would be worthwhile.

Among mental health problems, refugee trauma has been associated with low self-concept, shame, guilt, poor self-esteem, fear or anxiety, nightmares, feelings of helplessness, and unwanted or recurring intrusive thoughts about the traumatic event (Dye, 2018). DeBellis and Zisk (2014) identify exposure to war as one of several factors that may lead to trauma in children and may result in distress, posttraumatic stress disorder (PTSD), and posttraumatic stress symptoms (PTSS). Without appropriate interventions, these factors may create an individual who is socially maladjusted.

While most children are resilient and may cope well with these traumatic events, some children may use coping strategies that may be detrimental to their health and that of others. For instance, coping strategies may include alcohol and substance use and engaging in antisocial behaviors (DeBellis & Zisk, 2014). Avoidant behaviors may be used as ways of controlling painful and distressing re-experiencing of symptoms. Distancing or detachment may be used also to avoid or control a recurring event or thought. While this coping strategy may be appropriate for one situation, it may also be ineffective or inappropriate for another. It is important to use coping strategies that will positively impact one's psychological well-being.

I have learned that there is a reason for situations that we go through. Our experiences happen for a reason. Nothing goes to waste. Our experiences either benefit us or others or both. It is possible that I may have grown to be a selfish brat had I not experienced life of a refugee. My experiences have taught me empathy. I understand what it means to go hungry, to lack, to live with hopelessness, and to live under consistent threat. It is my hope that my story will give hope to the hopeless.

My experience as a preschooler under Mrs. Mkandla's guidance pulled me through my darkest hours as I would recite the rhymes and focus on the good times. Mrs. Mkandla may not have realized her impact on my childhood life, but I owe my mental well-being to her and that of my family, who provided a stable and sturdy foundation. I hope educators will be able to read this book and realize the impact of believing in their students and building their self-worth. That relationship carries that child through the darkest hours. This underscores the importance of providing a loving and sturdy foundation that helps a child fully develop to his or her potential.

The importance of social support cannot be underestimated. One should never walk alone. My family, immediate and extended, and my villages, both Sengezane and Sukwe, played a pivotal role in preparing me for what lay ahead. In my darkest hour, I would look back and focus on the positives, and darkness would turn into light. I would hope again.

My father retired from his job at a time when his family needed him the most. Like many families, he weighed his options, resigned from his position as a police officer, and sacrificed his family's and his well-being for the sake of the country. His early retirement led to his life spiraling out of control as he became an alcoholic. He was failing to cope with his new status. This, in turn, led to our mother's decision to move to Sukwe. By the time we moved to Sukwe, the "winds of change" had picked up speed, and a storm was already drenching the country before triumphantly ushering Zimbabwe's independence in 1980. These decisions, intended or unintended, led to family members joining the liberation struggle.

Tracing my family's roots from Ross Camp, to Sengezane, and to Sukwe, it seems we were being prepared for participation in the liberation struggle. Each member, and each village, contributed significantly to the struggle for independence. My brother Emmanuel missed being recruited by ZIPRA cadres many times. He evaded call-up by resigning from CABS but got called up while working for the railway company. He ended up being the integration officer, as he integrated the pre-independence armies into one national army at independence. My sister Thando was recruited at thirteen years of age but came back and was able to complete her education. Had these two gone to Zambia, our mother would have remained with no child at home since my sister Orpha passed on a few months after our recruitment. We also do not know if they would have survived. My family and I always wonder if my mother would have managed to live. My family, like many other Zimbabwean families, fought in different ways. Not everyone made it alive to enjoy the benefits of independence; some lives were lost so others would enjoy the benefits.

My experiences have made me a stronger, patient, tolerant, and resilient person. I believe that every difficult situation comes to an end. If the Zimbabwe War of Liberation came to an end, any difficult situation could come to an end.

One major lesson I have learned through my experience is compassion. Through various organizations, like United Nations Children's Fund (UNICEF), many people donated money, clothing, and various items to keep me clothed, sheltered, fed, educated, and with medical supplies. As a child refugee, there are many foods I detested. This could be the fact that I was eating or seeing those foods for the first time. Although I detested those foods, I was grateful for them. As I grew older, I realized and appreciated the sacrifice that other people from all over the world had made to give me my daily portion. They did not have to, but they understood the meaning of suffering and sacrifice. They had compassion and were motivated to go out of their way to provide for someone they did not even know. It is their compassion that kept me alive, well, and educated. Because I understand suffering, compassion is a virtue that I value.

The current United Nations High Commissioner for Refugees (UNHCR), the UN Refugee Agency's website, calls for a commitment to donate so that refugees rebuilding their lives could receive financial assistance, household essentials, and education. By donating, the agency can respond "quickly, effectively, and compassionately" to areas where needed. Compassion is a virtue to be desired. Without compassion, one walks alone and never understands the call of sacrifice.

As the world continues to have child refugees, it is compassion that will protect, feed, clothe, educate, and support them. As wars are waged, children become innocent victims. Compassion will understand the effects of war on children and address the plight of child refugees. Rebuilding one's life after being a refugee requires financial, social, and psychological support. Without compassion, those responsible for the welfare of these children will abdicate their responsibility. They will scorn the existence of child refugees, pretend they never existed, minimize the effects of wars on children, and disregard the plight of child refugees. They walk alone.

As VC and JZ children integrated into society, one wonders how each child settled and what type of services were available to help them rebuild their lives. Some came back home as orphans, others to single-parent homes, to poverty, and more fear and anxiety. As these former child refugees age and die, compassion will tell their story. Compassion will hear their story.

Many stories of ordinary Zimbabwean citizens have never been told and may never be told. But it is important to acknowledge that many people fought for the liberation of the country in various ways. Children in refugee camps were part of this fight and should never be forgotten or despised. Their story should be heard and told. Although they may feel neglected, they should never feel dejected. They played a role no one could have ever played. Their legacy should live on and be written in history books and be taught in schools.

Epilogue

During her first year, Lindiwe met challenges while trying to adjust to life in Zimbabwe. However, with the support of her family, Lindiwe was able to adjust as the years went by. She passed her Ordinary Level examination at the end of her fourth year in high school. As soon as her results were out, she enrolled at Hillside Teachers' College in Bulawayo. She trained as a high school teacher and taught isiNdebele at Manama High School in Gwanda for eight years.

While teaching at Manama, she sat for her Advanced Level and passed, qualifying her to enroll for her bachelor's degree in Education from the University of Zimbabwe. She graduated with a University Book Prize for best student in her cohort. After obtaining her bachelor's degree, she transferred from Manama to St. Columbus High School. Two years later, she joined her husband in the United States for her master's and doctoral degrees in Educational Psychology and Special Education. She is an associate professor of Education at Georgian Court University in the United States.

Lindiwe is married and lives with her family in the United States.

Bibliography

Bhebhe, Ngwabi. *ZAPU Military Strategy*. Gweru: Mambo Press, Gweru, 1999

De Bellis, Michael D., and Abigail Zisk. "The biological effects of childhood trauma." *Child and Adolescent Psychiatric Clinics of North America* 23 2 (2014): 185–222, vii.

Dias, Derek. *Distilling the Facts: 15 of Africa's Best Home-Made Brews*. https://afktravel.com/75517/distilling-facts-15-africas-best-alcohol-batches/ December 18, 2014. Accessed October 20, 2021.

Dubow, Saul. "Macmillan, Verwoerd, and the 1960 'Wind of Change' Speech." *The Historical Journal* 54. 4 (2011): 1087–1114doi:10.1017/S0018246X11000409.

Dye, Heather. "The impact and long-term effects of child-hood trauma." *Journal of Human Behavior in the Social Environment*. 28. 1–12: (2018). doi:10.108 0/10911359.2018.1435328.

Jennings, Arthur. C. "Land apportionment in Southern Rhodesia." *African Affairs* 34, (1935): 296–312, https/doi.org/10.1093/oxfordjournals.afraf. a100934. Accessed November 08, 2021.

Msimanga, Audrey. The role of birds in the culture of the Ndebele people of Zimbabwe. *Ostrich* 71, no.1 & 2: (2000): 22–24.

SAHA (2012). ZAPU through the Zenzo Nkobi's lens. https://www.saha.org.za/publications/zapu_ through_zenzo_nkobis_lens.htm Accessed December 2, 2021.

About the Author

The author is an associate professor of education at Georgian Court University in the United States. Dr. Lindiwe Magaya has presented numerous papers nationally and internationally, in the US and elsewhere. She belongs to the Division of International Special Education Services (DISES) and the Council for Exceptional Children (CEC). These platforms have provided opportunities to advance her work as an advocate for children with special needs and those marginalized. This is her first book.

CPSIA information can be obtained
at www.ICGtesting.com
Printed in the USA
BVHW091914160822
644714BV00008B/522

9 781685 566159